TRIUMPHANT TEAMS

Foul Football

TRIUMPHANT TEAMS

MICHAEL COLEMAN

www.michael-coleman.com

Illustrated by
Mike Phillips

Hippo

For all at Preston North End Football Club;

Commonwealth House, 1–19 New Oxford Street,
London WC1A 1NU, UK
A division of Scholastic Ltd
London ~ New York ~ Toronto ~ Sydney ~ Auckland
Mexico City ~ New Delhi ~ Hong Kong

Published in the UK by Scholastic Ltd, 2001

ISBN 0 439 99863 8

Typeset by TW Typesetting, Midsomer Norton, Somerset
Printed and bound by Cox & Wyman, Reading, Berks

6 8 10 9 7 5

Contents

Introduction 7

The 1870s: Winning Wanderers 10

The 1880s: Proud Preston 17

The 1890s: Victorious Villa 28

The Early Days Quiz 39

The 1900s: Nifty Newcastle 43

The 1910s: Brilliant Blackburn 52

The 1920s: Heroic Huddersfield 60

The 1930s: Awesome Arsenal 67

The Middle Ages Quiz 74

The 1940s: Powerful Portsmouth 78

The 1950s: Wonderful Wolves 87

The 1950s: Majestic Manchester United I 97

The 1960s: Terrific Tottenham 103

The Tempestuous Times Quiz 112

The 1970s: Lethal Leeds 116

The 1980s: Lordly Liverpool   127

The 1990s: Majestic Manchester United II   141

The Modern Game Quiz   155

INTRODUCTION

Some football teams are foul.

Other teams are so brilliant that they make all the rest cry, "Foul! They don't give us a chance!"

It's triumphant teams like these that you'll be reading about in this book. One team from every decade of English football history. Teams such as…
- the single most triumphant team, Liverpool
- the doubly triumphant Tottenham Hotspur team
- the trebly triumphant Manchester United team

Every triumphant team mentioned in this book won gallons of games, of course, but they didn't all go about it in the same way. Each had their own style, as you'll discover…

- like the team who were so triumphant that they liked to be photographed with their trophies *before* they'd even won them

- like the team who only became triumphant once they'd stopped packing their side with fat footballers
- like the team who had money thrown at them by opposing fans – not because they were so triumphant but because they were so unpopular

And, as always, we'll be triumphantly conferring our very own Foul Football awards on those who laid a brick or two on a team's road to stunning success. Awards like...

THE "I'M NOT LISTENING TO THAT SORT OF THING!" AWARD...

Albert Shepherd, Newcastle United (1908–11) who, if the Newcastle fans started yelling at him, would quickly shut them up – by walking off the pitch!

So don't just sit there, read on! Every page is a triumph!

THE 1870s: WINNING WANDERERS

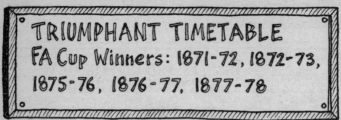

TRIUMPHANT TIMETABLE
FA Cup Winners: 1871-72, 1872-73, 1875-76, 1876-77, 1877-78

The Wanderers' claim to fame is that they won the FA Cup five times in seven seasons, the first time in 1872.

Question: Why hadn't they won it before? Was it because…?
a) Organized football hadn't started.
b) The Wanderers club hadn't been formed.
c) The FA Cup competition hadn't been invented.

WHAT ARE YOU WAITING FOR?

THE WANDERERS TO WANDER ALONG

Answer: c) The FA Cup was the first organized football tournament – ever! (For the full story read *The Phenomenal FA Cup*.) Until 1872, teams had only played friendly matches (even if they were games full of fouls; the rules weren't terribly organized in those days, either).

The Wanderers had been formed in 1859 by a group of ex-pupils from Harrow School but, because their first home pitch was close to Epping Forest, they'd originally called themselves Forest FC. (Well they *wood*, wouldn't they!) They changed their name to the Wanderers four years later when they decided to "wander" away to London and a new ground in Battersea Park.

Question: Relocating to Battersea Park was a good move, because more players lived in the area, but not perfect for another reason. Was it because...?

a) Matches had to stop if it was time for the park gates to be closed.
b) The changing rooms had no hot water.
c) The pitch was used as a loo by the residents of Battersea Dogs' Home.

Answer: a) So the Wanderers learned to start their games as early as possible and set about recruiting lots of top ex-public school and army players. Neatly kitted out in their colours of orange, violet and black, they so dominated the

FA Cup in its early years that their opponents must have "wandered" how any team could beat them!

Main Men
Charles Alcock

Alcock was the Wanderers' captain and the FA Cup was his idea as well! In fact, Alcock had so many ideas it was a wonder he wasn't called know-alcock. Maybe it was because his ideas were so good. As well as the FA Cup, Alcock was the first to think of international football matches and he captained England in an unofficial game against a Scotland XI. Ever watched England play Australia in a cricket test match? Test matches were his idea too!

The Right Honourable Arthur Fitzgerald Kinnaird

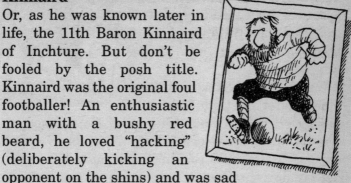

Or, as he was known later in life, the 11th Baron Kinnaird of Inchture. But don't be fooled by the posh title. Kinnaird was the original foul footballer! An enthusiastic man with a bushy red beard, he loved "hacking" (deliberately kicking an opponent on the shins) and was sad when the rules were changed to ban it. On one occasion, when he and Charles Alcock were on opposite sides in a match, Alcock asked what rules they were going to play by. "Oh, let's have hacking!" cried Kinnaird.

When it came to winning medals, the bashing Baron definitely knew how to hack it: he played in nine FA Cup Finals and was a winner five times.

Morton Peto Betts

Betts was the scorer of the first-ever FA Cup Final goal, a goal that gave Wanderers a 1-0 triumph against the Royal Engineers.

Was it described as a brilliant blockbuster? A scorching piledriver? A knock-out net-buster? No, newspaper reports were more genteel in those days – and anyway, Betts' shot couldn't have busted the goal net because they hadn't been invented yet. Neither had crossbars. The top of the goal was marked by a tape stretched between the goalposts, which is why the description of one of the most famous goals in history simply said...

"Betts scored with a well-directed kick under the tape."

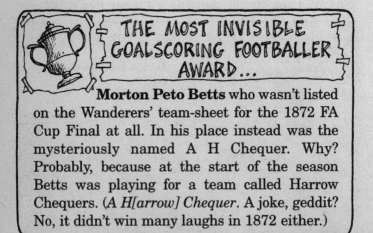

THE MOST INVISIBLE GOALSCORING FOOTBALLER AWARD...

Morton Peto Betts who wasn't listed on the Wanderers' team-sheet for the 1872 FA Cup Final at all. In his place instead was the mysteriously named A H Chequer. Why? Probably, because at the start of the season Betts was playing for a team called Harrow Chequers. (*A H[arrow] Chequer*. A joke, geddit? No, it didn't win many laughs in 1872 either.)

Wanderers won the first two FA Cup finals, missed out for a couple of years, then won each year from 1875 until 1877. Under the rules of the time, a team that won the competition three years in a row was allowed to keep the trophy. Maybe Charles Alcock had run out of ideas and didn't know what to do with it, because the Wanderers turned it down – on the condition that the rules were changed so that no other three-in-a-row team could win it outright either.

1877 was the end of the Wanderers' triumphant period. They didn't win the FA Cup again. Worse than that, a mere four years later the Wanderers had packed up altogether. Why?

a) They had no players.

b) They had no ground.

c) They had no money.

Answer: a) In a way they'd been too successful. They'd helped make football so popular that dozens of new teams were springing up … especially "Old Boys" teams made up of ex-pupils from different posh schools. The result: the Wanderers' players wandered off and joined their old school teams. For instance, their star, Lord Kinnaird, joined the Old Etonians (playing in another four FA Cup Finals with them). The country's first triumphant team quickly became a terrible tiddler and the club folded in 1881.

But an even bigger change was on the way than the spread of football amongst the gentlemen of the south of England. It was spreading like wildfire among the working people in the north of the country…

THE 1880s: PROUD PRESTON

TRIUMPHANT TIMETABLE
League Champions: 1888-89, 1889-90
FA Cup Winners: 1888-89

Preston North End were the first-ever team to manage the "Double" – winning the League Championship and the FA Cup in the same season. What's more, they did it without losing a match in the League or conceding a single goal in the Cup!

It was an amazing and unique achievement, coming just ten years after they'd played their first match. But what made Preston really proud was that in getting that far they'd had to overcome obstacles that would have stopped lesser teams.

Here's their troubled timetable:

5 October, 1878 After starting out as a cricket club, then adding a rugby section, Preston try their hands – well, feet mostly – at playing soccer.

They lose 1-0 to a team called Eagley. It isn't a bad start because, as the local newspaper reports:

THE NORTH END MEN WERE SOMEWHAT AT A DISADVANTAGE, NOT BEING ACCUSTOMED TO THE ASSOCIATION RULES

26 March, 1881 They hold a meeting and decide to give up rugby altogether. From now on, Preston North End are a soccer team. The players come straight out from the meeting to play local rivals Blackburn Rovers ... and lose 16-0!

THEY MAY BE PLAYING SOCCER BUT THEY'RE STILL GETTING RUGBY SCORES!

PRESTON NORTH END 0 0

BLACKBURN ROVERS 1 5 6

19 January, 1884 Preston enter the FA Cup for the first time. They reach the fourth round, but are expelled from the competition after a complaint by their opponents Upton Park, an amateur team from London.

Question: What have Preston done wrong?
a) Offered money to their own players.
b) Offered money to the Upton Park players.
c) Offered money to the referee.

Answer: a) Professionalism (paying your players money) was illegal. The FA rules said that players could only be given money that they'd spent getting to the game or lost by having to miss work.

The Preston manager, Major William Sudell, admits the offence – but says all the teams in the North do the same, and that it's only the London teams' well-off players who can afford to be amateurs.

This is not considered a good argument and Preston are banned from the following season's FA Cup competition as well.

5 December, 1885 The rules change. Professional players are allowed. Preston enter the FA Cup and reach the third round – only to be expelled again!

Question: What have Preston done wrong this time?

a) Offered money to their own players.

b) Offered money to their opponents.

c) Offered money to the referee.

Answer: a) again. The new professionalism rules say that clubs can only pay players if they were born, or live, within six miles of their ground. The fact that Preston's Geordie Drummond lives and works in Scotland breaks this rule!

24 March, 1888 Preston at last make it through to their first FA Cup Final. They're confident of triumph; so confident that they ask the referee if they can be photographed with the trophy before the match, while their kit is still clean! The referee refuses … and Preston's pride is pricked as they lose 1-2 to West Bromwich Albion in one of the greatest Cup-upsets of all time.

"The Invincibles"

The 1888–89 season began with a new competition: a Football League, with just 12 teams all from the North and Midlands. Preston were hot favourites. In fact, even though until then they'd only ever won the Lancashire Cup, everybody called them "The Invincibles".

How come? Because, in spite of their problems in the FA Cup, Preston had actually been beating most other teams out of sight in friendly matches. The season before they'd won 42 games in a row!

They'd gained their revenge for 1881 and belted Blackburn 7-0; demolished Derby County 8-0; exterminated Everton 6-0; battered Bolton 9-1; and, to top it all, on their run to the FA Cup final they'd hammered a team called Hyde by a record 26-0. In their 42-game winning streak, they'd scored 241 goals and let in just 45!

Preston duly proved they really were invincible. They ended the first-ever League season with these statistics:

PLAYED	WON	DRAWN	LOST	GOALS FOR	GOALS AGAINST
22	18	4	0	74	15

In the FA Cup, they beat Wolverhampton Wanderers 3-0 in the Final to go down in history as the first "Double" winners.

Main Men
David Russell

He was the "hard man" of the Preston team – and, as we're talking about a team who were masters at the (then perfectly legal) tactic of charging a goalkeeper out of the way if he looked like saving a  shot, that means as hard as nails! Sometimes Russell wasn't content simply to stop his opponent; in a match against Blackburn Olympic in 1886 he was reported to have chased his man the length of the pitch before booting him in the back!

He certainly wasn't a player to get too close to. One of his favourite tricks was trying to control the ball…

"…WITH A FOOT IN THE VICINITY OF AN OPPONENT'S EAR."

ATHLETIC NEWS, 1924

THIS IS GONNA HURT

Russell was also unique in one other way. He was the only Preston player who didn't have a moustache!

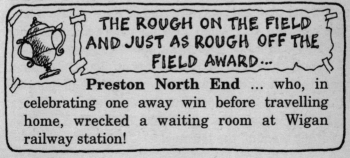

THE ROUGH ON THE FIELD AND JUST AS ROUGH OFF THE FIELD AWARD…

Preston North End … who, in celebrating one away win before travelling home, wrecked a waiting room at Wigan railway station!

Jimmy Ross

Ross was Preston's right-winger and an ace goalscorer. He was no softie either; in one game against Queens Park in Glasgow he committed so many fouls a large number of fans were waiting for him outside the ground afterwards – and they weren't after his autograph!

HOW CAN HE SIGN THAT?

They only left when they were told Ross had been arrested by the police for his dirty play – allowing the Preston player to be smuggled out and on to a train home.

KEEP YOUR HEAD DOWN TILL WE'RE CLEAR OF THE GATES

GATE 1

On the goalscoring front, one of Ross's feats hasn't been beaten yet. When Preston whacked Stoke City 7-0 in the first League season, Ross hit all seven goals. The only thing that took the edge off his achievement was that Stoke had two Preston reserves playing for them because they'd only turned up with nine players; one had missed the train and one had signed for another team on the journey!

John Goodall

wasn't known as "Johnny Allgood" for nothing. He was Preston's star player and he played for England too. Goodall not only scored goals, but played in a way that nobody  had before. Try his brightest idea next time you play. It's simple. All you do is this…

When somebody passes the ball to you … stop it and work out who best to pass it to.

Yes, in those days controlling the ball and passing it to one of your team-mates was really new! Until then, players would usually just blast the ball forward and run after it. Goodall's style of controlling the ball and passing accurately to his team-mates was called "scientific play"!

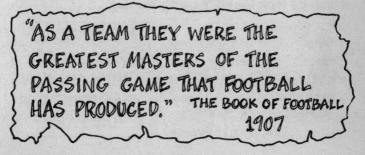

"AS A TEAM THEY WERE THE GREATEST MASTERS OF THE PASSING GAME THAT FOOTBALL HAS PRODUCED." THE BOOK OF FOOTBALL 1907

Goodall was an expert at playing another Preston innovation. You can try this one in the playground, too. Wait until somebody on your side has got the ball, then … don't run with them but *ahead* of them as you call for a pass.

Obvious? In the 1880s that was a new tactic too! Having developed closely with rugby, the usual style of passing was rugby-like, to the side. Opponents didn't know how to cope with Preston's new-fangled tactic of the through ball!

"The one passion of my life has been football – the most exhilarating game I know." – John Goodall.

Another talent that Goodall had isn't recommended for the playground, or anywhere else for that matter: in his later years he patiently trained a fox, which he took for walks with his dog.

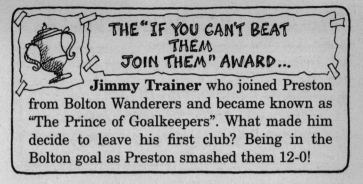

THE "IF YOU CAN'T BEAT THEM JOIN THEM" AWARD...

Jimmy Trainer who joined Preston from Bolton Wanderers and became known as "The Prince of Goalkeepers". What made him decide to leave his first club? Being in the Bolton goal as Preston smashed them 12-0!

Preston retained their League title in 1889–90. After that, they weren't so invincible and gathered a hat trick of runners-up places in the three seasons from 1890–93.

THE 1890s: VICTORIOUS VILLA

TRIUMPHANT TIMETABLE
League Champions: 1893-94, 1895-96,
1896-97, 1898-99, 1899-1900
FA Cup Winners: 1894-95, 1896-97

Although Sunderland – nicknamed "The Team of all the Talents" – became the first side to win the League three times, it was Aston Villa who were the most triumphant team of the 1890s. They won the League Championship five times and the FA Cup twice, bagging them both in the same year in 1897 which meant they'd achieved the League and Cup "Double" first managed by Preston North End. As you'll discover, Villa also *lost* the FA Cup twice: once on the pitch, and once off it!

The club's football history had begun in curious fashion. Their first-ever game had been against a rugby team, Aston Brook St Mary's. It had been a 15-a-side game, with the first half played as a rugby match (score 0-0) and the second half as soccer (1-0 to Villa)!

I THINK I SHOULD POINT OUT THAT YOU CAN'T ACTUALLY TACKLE LIKE THIS IN SOCCER

OH!

What's more, the football Villa had brought out for the second half hadn't even been their own – they'd rented it for 7p!

GET YOUR FOOTBALLS HERE, 7p A MATCH!

Since then they'd grown, joined the Football League, and even won the FA Cup in 1887. But by the 1890–91 season things weren't going so well for Villa. They finished in the bottom four in the League and were knocked out of the FA Cup in the second round. Their players were said to be more interested in something other than playing football. What?

A DANCING
B DRINKING
C GAMBLING

Answer: b) The players were sitting in pubs at all hours. In one incident a gang of them had been thrown out of a pub by police at 3 o'clock in the morning. And not just any old morning – on a Saturday morning, six hours before they were due to catch a train for a League game against Everton!

THE MOST ORIGINAL PRE-MATCH TRAINING TECHNIQUE AWARD...

Aston Villa. After their night out, the players travelled to Everton – and won 2-1!

29

The Aston Villa bosses shouldn't have been surprised at their boozing ball-players. Why? Because they'd put the drink in front of them in the first place. As an extra bonus for joining the club, they'd arranged for some of the team to become pub landlords!

They should have known that drink causes problems, even with a winning team. Only a few years before, in 1886–87, Villa had won the FA Cup for the first time, beating West Bromwich Albion 2-0 in the Final. But they could easily have been knocked out in their sixth-round match against Darwen. At half-time, with Villa 3-0 ahead, the President of a local rugby club had been allowed to parade a cup his team had won ... then fill it with champagne and offer it round to both teams! The Villa players staggered out for the second half, quickly conceded two goals, and only just sobered up to hang on for a 3-2 win!

More wobbly FA Cup moments came in the 1894–95 season as Villa reached the FA Cup Final for the third time – to meet West Bromwich Albion for the third time. If they'd had radio commentators in those days, here's how one might have described the start of the game:

After just 39 seconds Villa were 1-0 up! And after 90 minutes? Villa were still 1-0 ahead. That goal had been the only one of the game. Latecomers to the match – and there were lots of them, because the Final had just moved to a new ground at Crystal Palace – had missed the most important piece of the action! (Thousands of them probably threw away their most valuable memento of that day, too. One hundred years later, a copy of the one-penny match card listing the two teams was worth nearly £5,000!)

And then the club lost the Cup without kicking another ball! A Villa director, William McGregor, loaned it to a local boot and shoe shop to display in their window. And displayed it was – until some heel with no soul broke in on the night of 12 September 1895 and stole it. The trophy was never recovered and a new one had to be made, paid for with the money Aston Villa were fined for their carelessness.

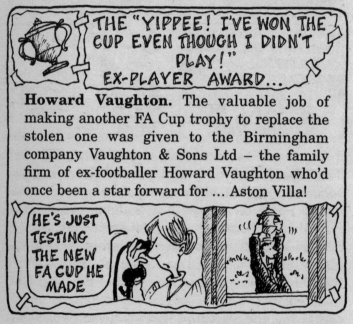

THE "YIPPEE! I'VE WON THE CUP EVEN THOUGH I DIDN'T PLAY!" EX-PLAYER AWARD...

Howard Vaughton. The valuable job of making another FA Cup trophy to replace the stolen one was given to the Birmingham company Vaughton & Sons Ltd – the family firm of ex-footballer Howard Vaughton who'd once been a star forward for ... Aston Villa!

HE'S JUST TESTING THE NEW FA CUP HE MADE

In the Football League, the team had become champions the season before, 1893–94. They repeated the trick two years later, in 1895–96.

And so to Aston Villa's finest season, 1896–97, in which they became the second team to win both the League Championship and the FA Cup in the same season (a feat not to be repeated for another 64 years). Saturday, 10 April was the most important day of the season for Villa. Why?

a) Because that was the day Villa won the League.

b) Because that was the day Villa won the FA Cup.

Answer: a) AND b) They triumphantly won both trophies *on the same day*!

By 10 April, 1897 – Cup Final day – Villa had built up a good lead in the League; so good that if second-placed Derby lost their next game, Villa would be champions. Back then, League matches were played on Cup Final day ... (no TV or radio in those days, remember, so football fans couldn't stay at home to follow the match) ... and Derby had a game. By the time Villa had beaten Everton 3-2 to win the Cup, Derby had lost to Bury to make them League Champions as well!

After one unsuccessful season, Villa were back on the triumphant trail in 1898–99, becoming League Champions on the last day of the season by lashing Liverpool 5-0.

They repeated the trick the following season – but only after another bottle battle! Suspicious that some of the players were drinking too much, the club took an unusual step...

Yes, the club actually hired a private detective to spy on their players to see if they were drinking too much. Three – one of them being Villa's star Scottish international defender James Cowan – were caught ... and promptly dropped for the team's FA Cup third-round replay against little Millwall Athletic.

Question: What happened next?
a) Villa won well and the players were transferred.
b) Villa suffered a shock defeat and the players were transferred.
c) Villa suffered a shock defeat and the players were brought back.

THE TOUGHEST OPPONENTS
BECAUSE IT TOOK NEARLY
FOUR MONTHS TO BEAT THEM
AWARD...

Aston Villa. On 26 November 1898, The
Wednesday (later Sheffield Wednesday) were
beating Aston Villa 3-1 when the game was
abandoned because it was too dark to continue.
The team were ordered to play the remaining
11 minutes of the match – on 13 March 1899!
Wednesday scored again to win 4-1.

Main Men
John Devey

Devey played for Villa
throughout their triumphant
period and twice for England. He
was Villa's captain, and had a
favourite trick. Try it:

- Sprint at top speed, but not
  towards the goal!
- Stop dead.
- Spin on your heels.
- Let fly with an unstoppable shot!

It worked brilliantly for dynamic Devey. He scored nearly 200 goals for his team!

Charlie Athersmith

Athersmith played on the right wing, and he also played for England, making his first appearance on the same day in 1892 as his Villa team-mate John Devey. Athersmith was fast, scored goals ... but, it seems, didn't always like playing in the rain. It's claimed that Athersmith once played a whole game sheltering under an umbrella!

HE PLAYS FOR THE RAINING CHAMPIONS!

James Cowan

Cowan was Villa's ace defender, a man who tackled even harder than he drank! It's a toss-up as to whom he gave a tougher time – his opponents or his club. Apart from the drinking escapade spotted by the private detective, he was also fined by the Villa bosses for another trick. During the winter of the 1895–96 season they allowed him to go home to Scotland to recover from an injury … only to discover that while he was supposed to be resting he'd been winning loads of money by running in Scotland's famous Powderhall Sprint race on New Year's Day!

> *For brilliancy and, at the same time, for consistency of achievement … the superiors of Aston Villa cannot be found.* – William McGregor, founder of the Football League (and Chairman of Aston Villa!)

THE MOST TRIUMPHANT TEAM NEVER TO WIN A TROPHY AWARD…

Corinthians FC. Corinthians played throughout the period dominated by the Preston and Aston Villa sides, but they never won a trophy – because their rules didn't allow them to enter competitions! They were a strictly amateur side, who played purely for fun. If they hadn't, *they'd* almost certainly have been the subject of the previous two chapters … because they were good!

In 1884 they beat Blackburn Rovers, the FA Cup holders, 8-1!

In 1888 they beat Preston, the double-winning Invincibles, 5-0!

In 1904 they beat Bury, the FA Cup Holders, 9-3!

Not surprisingly, Corinthians regularly provided well over half the players in the England team at this time.

They weren't just good at sport, they were good at being sporting as well. If they ever conceded a penalty, their goalkeeper would refuse to try and save it! They abandoned their rule of not entering competitions in 1922 and entered the FA Cup, but by then they weren't good enough to win it. What they never abandoned was the sportsmanship. In one match in the 1930s the referee didn't turn up so the Corinthians' captain played *and* refereed. At one point he even gave a foul against himself!

THAT'S IT! I'VE HAD JUST ABOUT ENOUGH OF ME, COMMITTING ALL THESE FOULS, I'M SENDING MYSELF OFF!

THE EARLY DAYS QUIZ

Try these questions on hilarious happenings between 1870 and 1899 … and see if you triumph!

1 Wolverhampton Wanderers took the FA Cup very seriously when they entered it for the first time in 1884: they did extra training … in their best clothes! True or false?

2 What took Blackburn Rovers over three years to create in the 1880s?
a) A ground big enough to hold 20,000 fans.
b) The longest unbeaten FA Cup run in history.
c) The design of their shirts.

3 The first-ever match between North London rivals Arsenal and Tottenham Hotspur took place in 1887 at Tottenham Marshes. Spurs were winning 2-1

when the game ended after just 75 minutes. Why?

a) One of the teams had another match to play that day.

b) It was too dark to carry on.

c) The pitch hadn't been reserved for the full 90 minutes.

TIME'S UP – OUR TURN

4 In 1888, Sunderland pulled out of the FA Cup competition after winning their way through to the fourth qualifying round. Why?

a) They couldn't raise a team.

b) They'd already arranged to play a friendly match on the same day.

c) They didn't like the team they'd been drawn against.

IS THIS THE WHOLE TEAM?

5 On 1 September 1891, when Wolverhampton Wanderers met Accrington, they scored what was probably the first penalty ever awarded in a League match – even though the League had been running for three years. True or false?

6 In 1892, Aston Villa's goalkeeper Jimmy Warner was in trouble with his club. He'd bet that Villa would lose that year's FA Cup Final. True or false?

7 What is Preston North End's goalkeeper Jimmy Trainer supposed to have worn during the second half of an FA Cup tie against Reading in 1894?
a) A pair of Wellington boots.
b) A raincoat.
c) Nothing but a big smile.

AARRGHH!

8 On 23 November 1896, Joe Powell of Woolwich Arsenal broke his arm in a game. What did he do just six days later, on 29 November?
a) He signed for Tottenham Hotspur.
b) He broke his other arm.
c) He died.

Answers: 1 True The extra training sessions were long walks. The players had to do them in their spare time. In those days, the fashion when out walking was to wear smart "walking-out" clothes – so the Wolves players actually trained in their grooviest gear! **2b)** In winning the FA Cup three years in a row, Blackburn stayed unbeaten from 20 November 1883 to 27 November 1886. **3b)** With Tottenham leading, 2-1. Arsenal had only themselves to blame for the defeat, though. They'd turned up late for the match. **4c)** They'd been drawn against their bitter local rivals Sunderland Albion. Rather than play them, they withdrew. (Maybe they were scared of being torn asunder-land?) **5 True** Penalties were introduced for the first time on that day. **6 False** (It was never proved to be TRUE, anyway.) Villa had surprisingly lost the Final 0-3 to West Bromwich Albion, with Warner's mistakes leading to all three goals. Warner admitted gambling on the game – but said he'd bet that Villa would win and that he wouldn't let any goals in! Whatever the truth was, he never played for Villa again. **7b)** It was raining hard and Trainer didn't have a lot to do. Preston won the game 18-0! **8c)** Powell's arm was in such a bad state it had to be amputated. He then contracted tetanus and blood poisoning. Six days after the accident poor Powell died, aged only 26.

THE 1900s: NIFTY NEWCASTLE

TRIUMPHANT TIMETABLE
League Champions: 1904-05,
1906-07, 1908-09
FA Cup Winners: 1909-10

The Newcastle United team of 1904–11 is rightly famous for winning the League Championship three times and the FA Cup once ... but it's almost as famous for losing another four FA Cup Finals during the same period!

The team had reached the top in little more than ten years, although they could have managed it even faster. When the Second Division of the Football League had been formed in 1892 Newcastle East End (as they were then called) had been invited to join – but had refused! Why?

a) They thought they weren't good enough.

b) They thought they were too good.

WELL, I DON'T THINK WE'RE GOOD ENOUGH, BUT WE'LL TELL THEM WE'RE TOO GOOD

GOOD! I THINK!

Answer: b) Newcastle turned down the invitation because they wanted to be put straight into Division One!

However they changed their mind just one year later and, in 1893–94 became a Second Division side. Five years later they'd made it into the First Division. They were on their way to a pulsating period of terrific triumphs – and terrible torments...

Triumph! Newcastle win the 1904-05 League Championship, scoring more goals than any other team and conceding fewer. They've also won through to the Cup Final and confidently expect to do what Preston and Aston Villa had done before them and achieve "The Double".
Torment! In front of over 101,000 spectators at the Crystal Palace ground they lose the Cup Final, 2-0 ... to Aston Villa!

Torment! Newcastle make it into the Cup Final the very next season, 1905–06, and lose again, 1-0 to Everton. Newcastle aren't the only ones who suffer, though. The 75,000 crowd at Crystal Palace have to put up with the torment of watching a terrible match. How terrible? In those days newspaper reporters sent their comments minute-by-minute back to their offices. Here's a three-minute lowlight from this match:

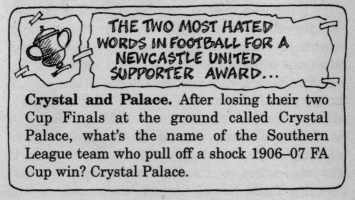

3:42 Newcastle get a corner.

3:43 Poor play in midfield.

3:44 The same.

3:45 Worse!

LIVERPOOL FOOTBALL ECHO, 21 APRIL 1906. TIME: 3:46 Dear Boss, I QUIT!

Triumph! It's 1906–7 and they're League Champions again. On their own ground they clock up 17 wins, 1 draw, and not a single defeat – at least, not in League games...

Torment! The only home match Newcastle lose in 1906–07 is in the first round of the FA Cup, when a tormenting tiddler of a team from the Southern League travel north and beat them 1-0!

THE TWO MOST HATED WORDS IN FOOTBALL FOR A NEWCASTLE UNITED SUPPORTER AWARD...

Crystal and Palace. After losing their two Cup Finals at the ground called Crystal Palace, what's the name of the Southern League team who pull off a shock 1906–07 FA Cup win? Crystal Palace.

Torment! 1907–08 sees a third Cup Final defeat, once again at Newcastle's hoodoo ground, Crystal Palace. After pulling off a record 6-0 semi-final win against Fulham, they crash 3-1 to Second Division Wolverhampton Wanderers.

Triumph *and* Torment! Newcastle take the League title for the third time in 1907–08, but only after tormenting their fans in the worst way possible. Injuries force them to play some reserves against Notts Forest, but the weakened team still win 4-0 ... and so the fit-again stars are left out for the next game against Newcastle's local and deadly rivals, Sunderland.

It's a ten-goal thriller. Trouble is, nine of the ten are scored by Sunderland as they charge to a crushing 9-1 win! It's the worst defeat ever suffered by a team in the same season they (thanks to a 16-match unbeaten run) win the League title.

Triumph! At last, an FA Cup Final win! It happens in 1909–10, with Newcastle beating Barnsley 2-0. So does that mean they'd finally beaten their crippling Crystal Palace problem? No, it doesn't. The win comes in a replay at Everton's ground, Goodison Park. Newcastle hadn't been able to win the first match at Crystal Palace. That had ended 1-1, with their goal late in the game coming as officials were getting ready to adorn the trophy with ribbons in Barnsley red!

Torment! Another FA Cup Final, and another miserable day at Crystal Palace. Newcastle draw 0-0 against Bradford City and this time they don't even win the replay either, going down 1-0 at Old Trafford, Manchester. They won't win the FA Cup again until 1924 ... by which time the Final will have moved to Wembley!

THE THICKEST EXCUSE FOR PLAYING ROTTEN GAMES AT CRYSTAL PALACE AWARD...

Newcastle United, who claimed that the grass was much thicker at Crystal Palace than at their home ground of St James's Park and messed up their smooth passing game.

Main Men
Colin Veitch

Colin wasn't your average footballer. For a start, he wore a bow tie. (Not when he was playing, of course!) When he wasn't playing footie for Newcastle

or England he liked nothing better than acting in Shakespeare plays or conducting an orchestra.

Veitch was a bit of a conductor for his team as well. When you play in a match, does your coach give you a team-talk at half-time? If so, then he or she is copying what Colin Veitch started with Newcastle.

FRIENDS, NEWCASTLE PLAYERS, COUNTRYMEN, LEND ME YOUR EARS!

WHY CAN'T WE JUST HAVE ORANGES AT HALF TIME?

Veitch carried on giving Newcastle team-talks even after he'd retired! He became a journalist and wrote regular articles saying how he thought Newcastle were doing. Sometimes he thought they weren't doing so well, and after one article Veitch was banned from the Newcastle ground!

Was he a goodie or a baddie, though? In the 1911 FA Cup Final replay, Veitch collided with Thompson of Bradford City. The referee waved play on, even though Thompson had been knocked out. As Bradford swept on to the attack, what did Veitch do?

a) He gave Thompson another whack to make the referee stop the game.

b) He ignored Thompson and raced back to help.

c) He stayed with Thompson to make sure he was all right.

Answer: c) What's more, he didn't even complain to the referee when Bradford's attack led to them scoring the winning goal.

Bill McCracken

McCracken was Newcastle's ace Irish international full-back. What the Newcastle fans thought of Veitch's sportsmanship in the 1911 Cup Final isn't known, but there's no doubt what the fans of every other club in the country thought of McCracken: they hated him! As the player once said cheerfully:

I WAS PELTED WITH MORE FRUIT THAN YOU COULD GET IN A GREENGROCER'S SHOP!

McCracken was so disliked because he was an expert at catching opposing forwards off-side. Until 1925 the off-side rule said that a forward had to have three players between him and the goal when he got the ball. McCracken didn't bother to tackle. He simply skipped upfield at exactly the right moment to leave the forward looking like a lemon! A master tactician.

Bill Appleyard and Albert Shepherd

This pair were Newcastle's goalscoring centre-forwards. Appleyard played until the end of the 1907–08 season, scoring 87 goals in 145 League games. His nickname was "Cockles", because before turning professional he'd been a fisherman. (That's probably why he was so good at finding the net!)

"EEL" GO FAR. LOOK AT THE WAY HE "SKATES" ROUND THE OPPOSITION!

Shepherd joined Newcastle from Bolton Wanderers – and wandering was definitely in his blood. Once, when the crowd started yelling at him during a game, he got so annoyed he wandered right off the pitch and back to the changing room!

Even one of his great moments with Newcastle – scoring the two goals which won the FA Cup replay against Barnsley – almost didn't happen. He'd been left out of the semi-final side because the club bosses thought he might be involved in gambling.

Question: So why was Shepherd brought back into the side for the Cup Final?
a) Another player insisted that Shepherd play.
b) Shepherd was found not guilty.
c) All the Newcastle players were found to be gambling.

Answer: a) The other player was Bill McCracken, who said that if Shepherd wasn't picked then he wouldn't play either! McCracken was good to Shepherd in the Final itself. Shepherd had already scored the first goal, and McCracken was Newcastle's penalty-taker so he should have taken the kick that gave them their second. Instead, to put Shepherd firmly back in favour, McCracken let Shepherd bang it in and go down in history as the scorer of the first-ever penalty in a Cup Final.

THE 1910s: BRILLIANT BLACKBURN

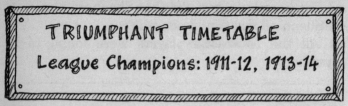

TRIUMPHANT TIMETABLE

League Champions: 1911-12, 1913-14

The Lancashire town of Blackburn produced two famous teams in the early days of football. Blackburn Olympic were the first side from outside London to win the FA Cup Final (in 1883), but Blackburn Rovers had been the first to actually reach the Final, losing 1-0 in 1882 to lively Lord Kinnaird's Old Etonians.

Their 1882 defeat had been unlucky, as even the Old Etonians' local Member of Parliament admitted at the after-game celebration dinner:

I WOULDN'T SAY THE WINNING GOAL WAS A FLUKE, FAR FROM IT, BUT IT WAS A HAPPY ACCIDENT

But Rovers had gone on to make up for that disappointment, winning the Cup five times in eight years, including a hat trick of wins between 1884 and 1886 (admittedly at a time when "The Invincibles" of Preston North End were being thrown out of the competition every five minutes!).

They'd never won the League Championship, though. The reliable Rovers' team of 1911–12 changed that. A mid-season surge of 17 games with only one defeat swept them to the title.

One of their first duties as champions was to play in the annual FA Charity Shield match. Nowadays, this game is played on the weekend before the Premiership season begins, and features the League Champions versus the FA Cup holders. In the 1912 match, though, Blackburn were pitted against different opponents. Who were they?

a) The Scottish League Champions.

b) The Southern League Champions.

c) The Second Division Champions.

Answer: b) The Southern League at that time contained all the big-name teams from London.

53

Blackburn beat Queen's Park Rangers 2-1, with the money raised going to a charity that had just been started. What was it?

a) The Battersea Dogs' Home.
b) The Professional Footballers' Benevolent Fund.
c) The Titanic Relief Fund.

Answer: c) The game was played in May 1912, instead of September, so that money could be put towards the fund for those who had suffered in the disaster when the huge liner hit an even huger iceberg in April that year.

I'VE GOT A SINKING FEELING WE'RE GOING TO LOSE THIS GAME

Two years later, in 1913–14, Blackburn Rovers were League Champions again. This time they started with a bang, winning their first five games and being unbeaten for the first ten, to go on and finish the season well ahead of Aston Villa in second place.

Champions or not, the team didn't have fans everywhere in Lancashire – especially in neighbouring Darwen. The two clubs hadn't been over-friendly for a while, so when they were drawn together in the semi-final of the little East Lancashire Charity Cup interest was high in

Darwen. Unfortunately, interest was a lot lower in Blackburn, and when Rovers sent along a reserve team – who were still good enough to run out 4-3 winners – the Darwen fans weren't deliriously happy. Armed with stones and lumps of grass, a mob of them waited until the Blackburn players left the ground, then pelted them until their tram came along. The only Rovers to escape were those who'd nipped out by a rear entrance and rapidly roved across a field before they were spotted!

An altogether more serious punch-up prevented the Blackburn team from going on to be an even more triumphant team – a punch-up called the First World War.

All professional football was suspended from 1915–19 with teams only playing in friendly matches and special war-time competitions.

Unfortunately for Blackburn their ground was closed as well, so their players had to go off to other teams for a game. This left Blackburn seriously short of men when special war-time football competitions started to take place. On one occasion, against Stoke City, they could only raise nine players. It's the only time in history that the reigning League Champions have been beaten 16-0!

Main Man

Blackburn had plenty of good individual players, of course, but they were a real team. Goals came from all over the pitch, although in 1913–14 a lot of them (28 in just 36 League games) were scored by Rovers' recent signing Danny Shea. His transfer from West Ham had broken the British record. He'd cost Blackburn a massive £2,000!

Bob Crompton

One player was the undisputed star of the Blackburn team – not just in their triumphant years, but before they started and after they were over. To see why, check out Bob Crompton's Crucial Career Credentials...

1897 Aged 17, he makes his first Blackburn appearance in a friendly. He plays centre-half and the local newspaper reports next day:

CROMPTON PLAYED A HARD GAME AND SHOWED PROMISE.

1900 A keen swimmer, he wasn't sure about becoming a professional footballer and insisted on finishing his apprenticeship as a plumber.

Now a regular in the team, Crompton switches to right-back. It's the position he'll play for the rest of his career.

1902 Crompton plays his first game for England, against Wales.

1912 Still playing, he's captain of the League Champions.

1914 Bob Crompton makes his final appearance in an England shirt, against Scotland. He's played 41 games, a record at the time. (It may not sound many, but in those days internationals meant playing Ireland, Scotland and Wales once a season. Nowadays, with European Championships and World Cups, Crompton's 41 would have turned into 120, easy!)

1920 He plays his last game for Blackburn. It's number 576. He promptly becomes a Blackburn director. It's a second sign (directors have to be well off!) that the rumours that Crompton's made lots of money on the side from his plumbing inventions could be true.

What was the first sign?

(a) HE OWNED A CAR
(b) HE OWNED A RACEHORSE
(c) HE OWNED A RESTAURANT

Answer: a) Hardly anybody owned a car in those days – especially footballers who only earned about £5 a week!

1928 It's Bob Crompton, Honorary – and winning – Manager. Taking over in 1926, he guides Blackburn to an FA Cup success at Wembley, 3-1 against Huddersfield Town.

1933 Always a quiet man, but with firm views, Crompton isn't prepared to listen to his players when they disagree with him. After a rebellion, he's voted out of the club after 34 years. He takes the news quietly and firmly, saying:

MY EXPERIENCE WITH THE ROVERS HAS BEEN A NICE ONE... I THANK YOU ALL

1938 Bob's back! Since his sacking, Blackburn have dropped into the Second Division and are on the verge of being relegated to the Third! Reappointed as manager, Crompton saves his team from relegation and, in the very next season, turns them into Second Division Champions!

1940 The outbreak of the Second World War – and the cancellation of the League competition – stops Crompton making a triumphant return to the First Division. But he guides Blackburn to a War League Cup Final at Wembley.

1941 Bob Crompton watches Blackburn play Barnsley. That evening, he collapses and dies. His life has ended in the most appropriate way possible: thinking about a Blackburn Rovers triumph. His team had won the game 3-2.

THE 1920s: HEROIC HUDDERSFIELD

Teams had won the FA Cup three years in a row before, but never the Football League Championship. That's the claim to fame of Heroic Huddersfield – they did it!

But then the club had always done things in threes, as the Huddersfield History for the first three years shows:

1908–09 In their first season Huddersfield finish a lowly fifteenth in the North Eastern League.

1909–10 Who cares? Not the Huddersfield bosses. They arrange for the club to join the Midland League for their second season. They finish in fifth place.

1910–11 Good enough? Good enough for the bosses to somehow persuade the Football League that the team's good enough. In only their third season, Huddersfield Town are elected to the Second Division! They finish thirteenth.

But that was the end of their climbing for a few years, until…

1919–20 Huddersfield finish second in Division Two and are promoted. (*And* reach the FA Cup Final, losing 0-1 to Villa.) The club that were about to make championship-winning history had made it to the First Division – without ever winning a League title!

THE TRIUMPHANTLY GETTING PROMOTED TO THE FIRST DIVISION AFTER NEARLY GOING BUST AWARD…

Huddersfield Town. In November 1919, the club were almost bankrupt. Their only hope seemed to lie in joining forces with another club in Leeds – and moving to their ground. The Huddersfield fans found this prospect so awful, they promptly raised enough money to keep the club going!

One other important event took place at this time: in March 1921, the Huddersfield team found themselves with a new manager. His name was Herbert Chapman – and for the next five years the fans loved him. After that, they really hated him!

They loved him ... when he led Huddersfield to a 1-0 triumph in the 1922 FA Cup Final, against Preston – even though it was one of the most boring finals ever, with just about the only entertaining moment in the whole match being the penalty Huddersfield scored to win them the match.

'ERE, WAKE UP! I THINK WE'VE GOT A PENALTY

A...WHAT?

They loved him ... in 1923–24 when Huddersfield became League Champions, and they certainly didn't care that they'd won the title by the slimmest margin ever – just a fraction of a goal. In those days teams level on points were separated by goal average (goals scored divided by goals let in). Huddersfield's goal tally of 60 scored and 33 let in was *just* better than Cardiff's 61 goals scored and 34 conceded! It wasn't all good news, though. The club's reserve team only managed to get second place in the Central League and they were beaten on goal average!

THE TRIUMPHANT TEAM
REWARD AWARD...

The Huddersfield Town Directors
who, at the end of the 1923–24 season,
rewarded each of their players with ... a canteen
of cutlery.

WE'RE REALLY
GOING TO CARVE
UP THE OPPOSITION
THIS YEAR

And the fans loved Herbert Chapman even more in 1924–25 when Huddersfield retained their title as League Champions, this time by a clear two points ahead of West Bromwich Albion.

But before the start of the 1925–26 season they hated him. Why? Because he'd left to become manager of Arsenal.

GET OUT!

I THOUGHT THEY LOVED ME!

At the end of 1925–26, though, they were laughing. Heroic Huddersfield had won the League Championship for a record third time in a row and they'd finished five fabulous points in front of their nearest challengers ... Herbert Chapman's new club, Arsenal!

I THINK I PREFER LAST SEASON'S RECORD

But the 1927–28 season was no laughing matter. Huddersfield had set another record. They'd become the first side to finish second in the League and lose the FA Cup Final (to Blackburn Rovers) in the same season. Talk about a "Depressing Double"!

And as for 1930 … It was, "Herbert Chapman, we hate you!" The golden period for Huddersfield Town was almost at an end. They made it to Wembley for the FA Cup Final, only to lose once more – 2-0 to Herbert Chapman's 'Appy Arsenal!

Main Men

Clem Stephenson

Clem was Huddersfield's captain for each of the League Championship seasons. He'd twice been an FA Cup winner with his previous club, Aston Villa, before Herbert Chapman signed him as his first new player – for £4,000! But why did Stephenson leave Birmingham-based Villa?

a) He objected to Aston Villa telling him where to live.

b) He didn't like Birmingham.

c) He didn't want to move house.

Answer: a), b) AND c). Villa had decided that all their players had to live in the Birmingham area, and Stephenson didn't want to move.

Alex Jackson was Chapman's last signing before he left. Jackson was a star Scottish international, a speedy goal-scoring winger nicknamed "The Laughing Cavalier" because of his skilful ball control, his eye for goal, and the

fact that he always seemed to enjoy the game whatever the result. England didn't think Jackson was very funny, though. When they played Scotland at Wembley in 1928, Jackson whacked in a hat trick as Scotland won 5-1!

Billy Smith

Smith played 520 games for Huddersfield between 1914–34 ... and was the main man in many of them. In the 1922 FA Cup Final against Preston, for instance, it was Smith who won his team's penalty. It was Smith's

feet that were pictured again and again by the new-fangled film cameras to prove he'd actually been fouled outside the area and it shouldn't have been a penalty at all. And it was Smith who got up to score the penalty, ignoring the Preston goalkeeper, James Mitchell, who was trying to put him off by doing chimpanzee impressions!

Smith also carved himself another place in football history on 11 October 1924. What was he the first player to do on that day?

a) Score direct from a corner.

b) Score three penalties in one match.

c) Score with a shot deflected by the referee's ear.

Answer: a) Until the summer of 1924 scoring direct from a corner hadn't counted. Billy Smith was the first player to manage it after the rule was changed. Who against? Arsenal!

THE TRIUMPHANT TEAM THAT SPENT MOST TIME IN THE HOUSES OF PARLIAMENT AWARD...

Huddersfield Town's 1920s team. Labour politician and twice Prime Minister Harold Wilson was a life-long Huddersfield fan and always carried a picture of the triumphant 1920s team in his wallet.

THE 1930s: AWESOME ARSENAL

TRIUMPHANT TIMETABLE

League Champions: 1930-31, 1932-33, 1933-34, 1934-35, 1937-38

FA Cup Winners: 1929-30, 1935-36

During the 1930s, Arsenal were Chapman's Champions. Not only did they repeat Huddersfield's feat of winning the League title three years in a row, they took it twice more and won the FA Cup a couple of times too.

Until then Arsenal hadn't won a thing, even though they'd been the first southern club to join the Football League in 1893. This lack of success may have had something to do with their peculiar player-purchasing policy.

Would your dad measure up as an Arsenal player? Try this test:

1 Does he weigh less than 11 stone? (69.85 kg) YES or NO?
2 Is he shorter than 5 ft 8 inches? (1.73 m) YES or NO?

I THINK HE'S TOO SHORT TO EVEN BE A BALL BOY!

ZZZ

3 Was he born in North London and/or does he live near Arsenal's ground? YES or NO?

4 Is he worth more than £1,000? YES or NO?

If you answered YES to question 3, but NO to questions 1, 2 and 4, then he would have been in with a chance (assuming he could also play football, that is!). Arsenal's policy in the 1920s was to buy tall, heavy, local players – but only if they didn't cost more than £1,000! (At that time the transfer fee record was over £5,000.)

Herbert Chapman stopped all that. He spent so much money that Arsenal soon became known as "The Bank of England Team". And as for the rest of the conditions ... his most successful purchase – for £9,000 – was Alex James, a player who was born in Scotland, was playing for Preston and was only 5 ft 5 inches (1.63 m) tall! A Scottish international, James scored twice in the 1928 5-1 defeat of England.

THE MOST SUCCESSFUL MANAGER AT PUTTING HIS TEAM ON THE MAP AWARD...

Herbert Chapman of Arsenal. In 1932 he talked the London Electric Railway Company into changing the name of the tube station closest to their ground from Gillespie Road to ... Arsenal.

'ARSENAL' STATION

D'YOU THINK THEY'D CHANGE OUR STATION TO DOG AND DUCK DIVERS?

Arsenal's triumphs under their new manager ended up being uncannily similar to those of Herbert Chapman's previous team, Huddersfield.

In the 1931–32 season they also completed a "Depressing Double", coming second in the League and losing the FA Cup Final.

Then, just like Huddersfield, between 1932 and 1935 awesome Arsenal became League Champions three times in a row. It was a team triumph that, once again, the famous manager wasn't around to see.

- Huddersfield had won their third League title after he'd left them to become Arsenal manager…
- and Arsenal were only halfway towards their hat trick of championships when, in January 1934, Chapman suddenly died.

The team he'd left behind just went on winning and banging in the goals. In 1934–35 they won their third title by scoring 115 goals – 25 more than any other team in the First Division.

Even their goalkeeper, Frank Moss, got on the score-sheet once. Injured in their match against Everton, he came back to play on the wing (no substitutes in those days, remember) – and scored Arsenal's second goal in a 2-0 win!

What was the secret of this goal-grabbing glory? A new tactic, of course, just like the triumphant teams before them. This one involved the Arsenal wingers. Up till then, this is what a winger tried to do:

- Stay on the touchline until he got the ball.
- Then race down the touchline (beating any full-backs in the way) until he couldn't go any further because he'd reached the corner flag.
- Then cross the ball for somebody else to bang into the net.

But this is what an Arsenal winger would do:

- Stay on the touchline until he got the ball.
- Then race *inside* his full-back until he got within shooting distance.
- Then bang the ball into the net himself.

Even when other teams started to copy their successful strategy, Arsenal's triumphant team were still good enough to win trophies. In 1935–36 they won the FA Cup Final again, beating Sheffield United 1-0, and in 1937–38 they became League Champions for the fifth time in the decade.

Main Men

The Arsenal squad of the 1930s was overflowing with main men. How overflowing? Well, in 1934 England played the reigning World Cup holders – Italy – and seven of the team that won 3-2 were Arsenal players!

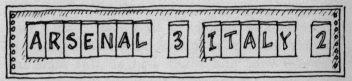

Alex James

The little Scots player Herbert Chapman had bought not long after becoming Arsenal manager had moved from Preston, where he'd been so much the main man that for a while Preston had been called "Alex James and ten others".

Nicknamed the "Wee Wizard", everything about James was short ... except for his shorts! They were so baggy and long they almost touched the tops of his socks!

Question: Why did Alex James say he wore long shorts?

a) To give him room to bend down while he was dribbling.

b) To keep his knees warm.

c) To put defenders off with the sound of them flapping as he ran.

Answer: b) Well, that's why he *said* he knee-ded them!

71

James was Arsenal's "schemer" – and not just on the pitch. Before the 1930 FA Cup Final against Huddersfield he told Cliff Bastin, the Arsenal left-winger, that if they got a free-kick in the opposition's half he would play it quickly to him, run for a return pass, and have a shot. It worked, too! After 16 minutes James was fouled, played the quick free-kick exactly as he'd said ... then took Bastin's return pass to score Arsenal's first goal in their 2-0 win. And where had all this scheming taken place? On the coach travelling to Wembley!

Cliff Bastin

Arsenal's goal-scoring winger hadn't joined Arsenal as a goal-scoring winger at all. He was stunned when manager Herbert Chapman told him that's the position he wanted him to play – because Bastin hadn't played on the wing since he was nine years old!

Question: Cliff Bastin's nickname was "Boy". Why?

a) Because he went on and on about not having played on the wing since he was a boy.

b) Because his favourite saying was, "Boy oh boy!"

c) Because he won so much as a young player.

Answer: c) By the time he was 21, Bastin had won a League Championship medal, an FA Cup winner's medal ... and played for England.

Ted Drake

Ted joined Arsenal in time for the 1934–35 season. His job was to score goals, and he did – 42 of them in that first year. His most remarkable feat came in the following season, though. On 14 December 1935 awesome Arsenal whacked atrocious Aston Villa 7-1 ... with Drake scoring *all* his team's goals!

Question: How many shots did Ted Drake have during the game?

Answer: a) 7 went in – and the other hit the bar!

THE MIDDLE AGES QUIZ

More questions to try, this time about entertaining events from 1900 to 1939. Can you top the League?

1 Sheffield United's goalkeeper in 1900 was Bill "Fatty" Foulke, who weighed over 20 stone (127 kg). When people called him names he had this reply all ready. Fill in the missing word.

I DON'T CARE WHAT YOU CALL ME AS LONG AS YOU DON'T CALL ME LATE FOR XXXXX

2 What did Everton and Liverpool share for the first time on 1 September 1904?
a) A ground.
b) A match-day programme.
c) An orange football.

WE PLAY WITH AN ORANGE BALL

I QUITE LIKE THIS BALL

OR THE RED ONE?

3 In 1908 Wolverhampton Wanderers beat Newcastle United in the FA Cup Final. When they got back home, the triumphant team's celebration tour of the town was to include a stop at a church. True or false?

4 What was Huddersfield Town's match mascot for their first-ever League game at the beginning of the 1910–11 season?

a) A blue and white goat.

b) A black and white zebra.

c) A red and white duck.

5 Frank Barson, Aston Villa's toughest defender in this era, was such a cruncher he even got sent off in another Villa player's testimonial match. True or false?

6 What present did triumphant Herbert Chapman receive from the Huddersfield Town staff in 1925 when he left to take over as manager of Arsenal?

7 In 1930, Manchester United acquired a new player, Hughie McLenahan, from Stockport County. In payment they gave Stockport County three … what?

a) Sets of football shirts.

b) Freezers of ice cream.

c) Old pence.

8 In 1939, before their Cup Final against Portsmouth, Wolverhampton Wanderers manager Frank Buckley gave his players injections of vitamins extracted from monkeys! True or false?

Answers: 1 – Lunch! **2b)** It was called "The Everton and Liverpool Football Programme" and cost one old penny (less than 1p). **3 True.** One of the Wolves' players was Kenneth Hunt, who was later to become a Church of England vicar. The stop was to have a celebratory cup of cocoa and lump of cake with Hunt's dad, the vicar of St

Mark's Church. In the event the crowds stopped the team getting there, so the cocoa had to go-go. **4a)** ...but don't report them to the RSPCG – the goat was only wearing a blue and white cover. Exactly why isn't too clear – Huddersfield played in red at that time! (They only changed to their familiar blue-and-white stripes in 1913.) **5 False.** He got sent off in his *own* testimonial match! **6a)** It must have come in handy for working out how many trophies his teams won. **7b)** McLenahan was an amateur, so it wouldn't have been legal to pay a transfer fee for him. Instead, Stockport made some money by selling the ice cream at a fund-raising bazaar! **8 False** ... although Buckley *had* claimed that he'd done just that. He later said it was a publicity stunt, but nobody could be completely sure. His team had played like a bunch of monkeys and been whacked 4-1!

THE 1940s: POWERFUL PORTSMOUTH

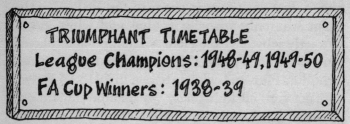

Portsmouth's triumphant team, like Blackburn's in the 1910s, might have been even more triumphant if they hadn't had a wicked war get in the way. In Portsmouth's case it was the Second World War, which caused the Football League and FA Cup competitions to be cancelled between 1939 and 1945, just as the team had lifted their first major trophy.

In 1939, Portsmouth had battled through to play hot favourites Wolverhampton Wanderers in the FA Cup Final. Was their run the result of a tremendous team performance ... or was it luck? The way the Portsmouth contingent carried on, they must have thought it was a bit of both.

a) Their manager, Jack Tinn, had insisted on wearing his lucky spats (clip-on cloth protectors that saved the tops of his shoes from getting muddy) for every round.

b) One of his players, Freddie Worrall, had insisted on being the player to put them on for him ... always the left first, then the right.

c) As for Worrall himself, when he ran on to the Wembley pitch he was a one-man good-luck charm, with...

● A small horseshoe in his shorts pocket.
● A sprig of heather down each sock.
● A tiny white elephant pinned to one of his tie-ups.

MAYBE I SHOULD HAVE LEFT OUT THE HORSESHOES

CLANG! CLONK!

Lucky or not, Portsmouth won the match 4-1 and held on to the FA Cup for the next seven years until it was played for again in 1946.

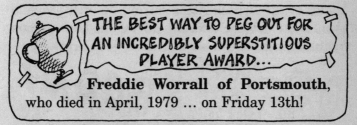

THE BEST WAY TO PEG OUT FOR AN INCREDIBLY SUPERSTITIOUS PLAYER AWARD...

Freddie Worrall of Portsmouth, who died in April, 1979 ... on Friday 13th!

After the war, Portsmouth took a while to get back into the swing of things. The same can't be said for their superb supporters.

Everything was in short supply. You couldn't buy as many clothes as you wanted, only what you were allowed. Special coupons were issued and you had to hand them over with your money. When your coupons were gone, that was it until it was time for more to be issued. What did the Portsmouth fans do with some of their precious coupons? They handed them over to the club so that they could buy a new set of football shirts for the team!

What's more, they turned up to support their team in huge numbers. In 1946–47 a crowd of 10,000 turned up ... to watch the reserve team! Their most famous supporter, Field Marshall Montgomery – leader of the British Army during the war – would even write letters offering advice on how a good football team should be just like a good army.

And, in 1948–49, the team didn't let their fans down. Exactly 50 years after they'd been formed in

1898, Portsmouth's triumphant team won the League for the first time in their history, completing the season without a home defeat.

They even stood a good chance of achieving the League and FA Cup double, only to be on the receiving end of a shock themselves. Drawn against Leicester City of the Second Division, Portsmouth were favourites to make the Final but lost the game 3-1. Are you a goalkeeper? Here's how NOT to deal with crosses coming over from the wing...

That was the method used by Portsmouth's goalkeeper Reg Butler. Unfortunately, and with Leicester 2-1 ahead, their young forward Don Revie had spotted Butler doing this – and he was ready for the next time. He waited for Butler to palm it down, then nipped in to get it first and score Leicester's crucial third goal!

Even so, the players were handsomely rewarded for what they'd achieved. The club gave each of them ... a £10 shopping voucher! (Nowadays you'd be lucky to get two pairs of pants for that, but in those days £10 was quite a lot.)

Portsmouth won the League Championship for the second time in succession a year later, 1949–50, beating old rivals Wolverhampton Wanderers into second place on goal average. A team without any international players at that time had triumphed again.

So, what was their secret? Were they Powerful Portsmouth – or Pretty Portsmouth? Weigh the evidence for yourself...

EXHIBIT A:
AS EARLY AS 1926, PORTSMOUTH HAD
BEEN ACCUSED OF...

...persistent playing of the man, not
by the shoulder but by the arm and the
foot, cutting him off by the knee and
the ankle, with the ball left severely
alone...

LANCASHIRE
DAILY POST

EXHIBIT B:
IN THE 1939 CUP FINAL, JIMMY GUTHRE-
PORTSMOUTH'S CAPTAIN THAT DAY - GROWLED IN
THE EAR OF THE WOLVERHAMPTON PLAYER HE'D
JUST FLATTENED THAT THE NEXT TIME HE'D
FIND HIMSELF IN THE ROYAL BOX!

EXHIBIT C:
NEWSPAPER REPORTS OF THE 1948-49 TEAM
HAD SAID THAT THEY WERE...
Too robust and (their) tackling inclined to
be clumsy.

EXHIBIT D:
THE TEAM'S NEWSPAPER NICKNAME
WAS: **THE IRON MEN OF
PORTSMOUTH**

Made up your mind yet? Then don't! Wait until you've read about their two main men...

Main Men
Jack Froggatt

Jack was a butcher, but no, not on the field! He worked in his dad's butcher's shop before he became a professional footballer. Then he became a flying winger (except during the Second World War; then  he just flew ... as a pilot in the Royal Air Force) and scored plenty of goals.

FROGGATT WILL HELP US WIN THE CUP THIS YEAR

YEAH! AND PIGS MIGHT FLY!

1949 was a good goal year for Jack. In April he scored a hat trick of headers from the left wing in Portsmouth's 5-0 win against Newcastle, and in November he played his first match for England – and scored again in a 9-2 victory over Northern Ireland. But, by 1951, Froggatt wasn't on the wing any more. Was he injured? No, somebody else was – Portsmouth's regular centre-half. So Jack Froggatt took his place ... and played so well that he not only stayed there for good, he was picked for England in that position as well!

Pleased? You bet he was. No wonder his nickname was "Jolly" Jack Froggatt!

Jimmy Dickinson

Portsmouth's other main man had a nickname, too: "Gentleman Jim". And no wonder. He was a midfielder who played 764 games for Portsmouth ... and wasn't booked or spoken to by the referee once! (A lot of today's defenders seem to do it the other way round – they get spoken to 764 times in one game!) He also played 48 games for England and didn't cause the referee any trouble in those games either.

Dickinson was a calm, stylish and unhurried player. Some of these qualities must have rubbed off on the other Portsmouth players, because Dickinson once said:

IF WE WERE A GOAL DOWN, EVEN TWO, NOBODY WORRIED. WE JUST GOT ON WITH THE JOB, FOUGHT BACK - AND USUALLY WON!

He was tough enough, though. On 20 April, 1949, with Portsmouth fighting to win the League title, Dickinson injured his head and needed stitches. The cut still hadn't healed properly when he ran out three days later for a deciding match against Bolton

85

Wanderers and it soon opened again. Off went Jim for more stitches. No good. So for the rest of the game he ran around, unable to head the ball, holding a blood-soaked cloth to his cut ... and played brilliantly as Portsmouth triumphed 2-1 and became Champions!

So – powerful Portsmouth or pretty Portsmouth? The real answer is, like all triumphant teams, they were a bit of both. After all, with Jolly Jack and Gentleman Jim in their side they couldn't have been totally foul, could they?

THE 1950s: WONDERFUL WOLVES

TRIUMPHANT TIMETABLE
League Champions: 1953 - 54,
1957 - 58, 1958 - 59
FA Cup Winners: 1959 - 60

Wolverhampton Wanderers, or simply The Wolves, were the side nobody fancied playing throughout the 1950s – and, for the first time, that meant teams from Europe as well as England. One of Wolves' claims to fame is that they were great at teaching "continental" club sides a lesson in how to play football "the English way".

This would have been great news to two of Wolves' nineteenth-century founders – because they'd been teachers themselves. Their names were Jack Baynton and Jack Brodie, and they'd been pupil-teachers (senior pupils who helped the school's headmaster) at St Luke's School in the town. In fact, you might think they'd been perfect teachers in every way. Measure your teacher against the qualities of the two Jacks:

● They were good footballers themselves.
● They were really enthusiastic about football and encouraged the boys to play it non-stop.
● They were great at teaching football.
● They were totally useless at teaching all the other subjects!

As St Luke's Headmaster, Mr Barcroft, wrote on 10 May 1879:

St Luke's Report ...

The teachers have not attended to their duties well this week. I have had to correct Baynton and Brodie several times within a few hours of neglect of duty; I found Brodie on the floor and boys laughing at him! Mr Barcroft

They may not have been much good at controlling classes but Baynton and Brodie were great at controlling a football. St Luke's FC quickly became Wolverhampton Wanderers and were one of the founder members of the Football League when it kicked off in 1888.

But ... as the 1953–54 season kicked-off, Wolves still hadn't won it! They'd lifted the FA Cup, most recently in 1949, but not the League title. All that was about to change. By the end of the season Wolves were Champions. Their most successful period had begun. Over the next eight seasons they won the League twice more (in 1957–58 and 1958–59) and were only once placed outside the top three. Added to that record, they also won the FA Cup in 1960.

Question: What was the secret of their success? How many of these facts about Wolverhampton Wanderers are true?

1 Their manager never used rude words.

2 Most of their players had been born near Wolverhampton.

3 The team hardly ever changed.

4 Wolves' captain was also captain of England.

5 Their tactics were called "kick and rush".

Answer: They're all true, and they probably all helped in different ways.

1 Their manager, Stan Cullis, didn't approve of bad language and never used it. He didn't have to, he knew how to shout – he'd been a Sergeant-Major in the army!

2 All but four of the Wolves team had been born in the area. (So maybe Arsenal's tactics before the 1930s weren't completely mad!)

3 Their team was amazingly similar week after week; eight of the players appeared in all three of the Championship-winning sides.

4 Wolves' captain, Billy Wright, certainly was captain of England – 90 times in total. But he had plenty of help. Seven of the Wolves team played for their country. In fact, in the 1958 World Cup, England's half-back line read: *Clamp, Wright, Slater* – all Wolves players!

5 "Kick and rush" was how the newspapers described Wolves' tactics. Wolves' manager, Stan Cullis, explained it in a simpler way:

I BELIEVE THAT THE QUICKER THE BALL IS IN THE OPPOSITION PENALTY AREA THE MORE LIKELY WE ARE TO SCORE GOALS

And that's exactly what Wolves did. Here's one of their classic three-touch goal-scoring moves to try out in the playground:

1ST TOUCH A DEFENDER BELTS THE BALL TOWARDS THE OPPOSITION CORNER FLAG...

BOOT!

2ND TOUCH A FAST WINGER CATCHES UP WITH IT AND BELTS IT INTO THE GOAL MOUTH...

SMACK!

3RD TOUCH A FORWARD OR MIDFIELD MAN RACES IN AND WHACKS IT INTO THE NET!

BLAST!

Simple – but only if you've got the players to do it. Wolves had them. What's more, they could keep on doing it for the whole game, as some famous European sides discovered...

Wolves, Champions of the World!

During the 1950s Wolves didn't just triumph against the other League teams, they also regularly took on top foreign teams in floodlit mid-week friendly matches as well. Playing evening games wasn't done that often in those days, so Wolves were definitely leading lights in this way!

Their two biggest successes came at the end of 1954. Both showed how Wolves' tactics had a habit of paying off in the end.

- In November they met the Russian team Moscow Spartak. At half-time the score was 0-0; after 60 minutes it was 1-0 to Wolves; after 87 minutes it was still 1-0 to Wolves ... but when the whistle went to end the game, it was 4-0 to Wolves. They'd scored three goals in the last three minutes.

- Then, in December, Wolves played the brilliant Hungarian side, Honved. How brilliant? Very brilliant. Five of their players had been in the Hungarian teams that had annihilated England 6-3 and 7-1 only the season before! At half-time, Wolves were 0-2 down...

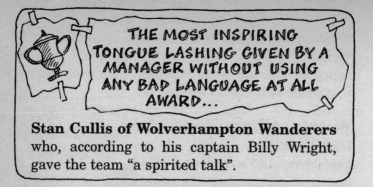

Whatever Cullis said, it worked. Wolves scored three goals in the second half to run out 3-2 winners. As the press said the next day:

> *Wolves can rightly proclaim themselves club champions of the world!* Daily Mirror, 14 Dec 1954

Stan Cullis tried doing just that. Nobody outside England believed him, but they didn't yet have a way to prove him wrong. The following year, however, the European Champions Cup was instituted, and when Wolves entered the competition in 1958–59, and again the following season, they didn't do all that well. (Their "kick and rush" style had now become obsolete.) Still, Wolves' unofficial European successes had caused people to think.

Main Man

Although the Wolves team of the 1950s was packed with internationals, one of them was recognized as *the* main man...

William Ambrose "Billy" Wright

Are you a sharpshooter, but one who's seriously short? Or are you a dithering dribbler who can't quite decide which is your best position on the pitch? If you answered "yes" to either of those questions then Billy Wright should be your hero!

THE MUM KNOWS BEST AWARD...

Billy Wright's mum. When Billy's headmaster suggested he should join a football club, Wright himself fancied Arsenal. His dad preferred Aston Villa. But his mum said Wolves. So that was that!

YOU'RE GOING TO WOLVES

WOLVES SOUNDS GOOD

SOUNDS VERY GOOD

Wright wasn't tall at all – just 5' 8" (1.73 m). When he joined the Wolves ground staff in 1937 the manager, Frank Buckley, tried giving him jobs he thought might make him grow ... like picking up the rubbish from the stands and collecting grass clippings! Wright didn't moan when the pitch was mown but, a year later, he still hadn't grown!

Question: What did Buckley do?

a) Send him away.

b) Keep him on as a grass collector and stand cleaner.

c) Promote him.

Answer: a) then c) Buckley told Wright he was still too short to be a footballer and sent him home – only to call him back again because one of his ground staff had told him he was a good worker. So Wright ended up being "promoted". Along with another titchy player, a winger named Jimmy Mullen, Wright became the Wolves' bath scrubber and kit packer!

That's how Billy Wright got his first taste of FA Cup Final atmosphere. When Wolves went off to Wembley to play (and lose to) Portsmouth in 1939 it was Billy Wright and Jimmy Mullen who'd packed the hamper carrying their Cup Final kit.

Wolves won their way back to Wembley ten years later, meeting Leicester City in 1949. They won 3-1, and this time Wright had a different carrying job. He was the player who had to carry the FA Cup down from the Royal Box – because he was now Wolves' captain! (And who was in the team as well? Jimmy Mullen.)

What had happened in those ten years? Firstly, he'd kept on playing and trying to improve his game, doing so well that Wolves manager Buckley changed his mind and signed him on as a player. But, more importantly, Buckley had suggested he try a different position: midfield instead of up in the forward line. Wright had given it a go – and he'd found his position!

It was the change that turned Billy Wright into one of the best players ever to wear an England shirt. Apart from his successes with Wolves Wright went on to win a (then) record 105 caps for England, 90 of them as captain.

Question (to discover how carefully you've been reading this book!): Billy Wright's 100th appearance for England was obviously special because no player had ever clocked up a century of appearances for his country before. But why was his 42nd appearance for England also important?

Wright didn't make a fuss during a game and he didn't make a fuss when he stopped playing either. He simply came off the field after a Wolves practice match in 1959 and said that he'd just played his last game.

Billy Wright died in 1994, but Wolves' fans still see him at every Wolves' home game – there's a statue of him outside the ground!

THE 1950s: MAJESTIC MANCHESTER UNITED I

The triumphant team that died

A new competition had started in 1952–53. Called the FA Youth Cup, it was a knock-out competition for under-18 teams. Doing well in this competition quickly became a good sign that a club had a triumphant team in the making.

In its first two seasons, for example, Wolverhampton Wanderers' Youth team were losing finalists. Five years later, the club were League Champions!

Question: If Wolves were twice *losing* finalists, from which clubs did the two *winning* youth teams come?

Answer: Manchester United ... and Manchester United. And while we're at it, here are the winning clubs for the following three years as well: Manchester United, Manchester United and Manchester United. Yes, for the first five years of its life, the FA Youth Cup was a one-team tournament.

So in the 1950s did Manchester United, like Wolves, have a triumphant team in the making? They certainly did.

In 1955–56 they stormed away with the League title, finishing 11 points ahead of their nearest challengers. (This was when a win was worth two points, remember. Nowadays, with a win earning three points, the Manchester United lead in 1955–56 would be equivalent to 16 points.)

The following year, 1956–57, wasn't quite so good. They only won the League by eight points! On the way they'd scored 103 goals, and reached the FA Cup Final where they lost to Aston Villa (after their goalkeeper was carried off and they'd played most of the game with ten men).

Manchester United's manager was one of their ex-players, a Scot named Matt Busby. So, with such a young side, it didn't take long for the newspapers to give them a nickname: the "Busby Babes".

HE'S A WONDERFUL DRIBBLER, MR BUSBY!

BURP!

Other teams were wondering – and worrying! – just how good Busby's team could get. And not only teams in the Football League. The new European Champions Cup had begun in 1955–56 and clubs throughout Europe were soon running into the Busby Babes – and bawling about it!

After winning the League in 1955–56, Manchester United became the first English team to enter a European tournament in 1956–57. They were drawn against the Belgian Champions Anderlecht in the first round, won the first leg 2-0 in Belgium … then took the second leg 10-0 in Manchester!

THE MOST SENSIBLE
SELECTION SUGGESTION
AWARD...

Jef Mermans, captain of Anderlecht, who said after the Busby Babes had annihilated Anderlecht,

WHY DON'T THEY PICK THE WHOLE SIDE FOR ENGLAND?

In the end they were knocked out in the semi-finals by the eventual winners, Real Madrid. But, as League Champions again, the Busby Babes were back in Europe the following season, 1957–58. And, again, they'd stormed through to the semi-finals after beating Red Star Belgrade 5-4 on aggregate. They'd won 2-1 in Manchester and, on 5 February 1958, they drew 3-3 in Belgrade.

It was the last match that team ever played together.

At just after three o'clock in the afternoon the next day, 6 February 1958, their plane crashed. On the way home to Manchester it had landed at Munich airport to refuel. The weather was awful. Snow and ice were all over the runway. Twice the plane tried to take off and had to stop. The pilot decided it was safe to try again. But the plane never left the ground. Instead it overshot the runway, went through a fence, then hit a house and a shed. There was an explosion.

In that moment a team died.

Main Men

Of the 40 people on board that aeroplane, 21 died. Eight of those who lost their lives were Manchester United players...

Geoff Bent
A newcomer at left-back, Geoff only played 12 games. Age: 26.

Roger Byrne
An attacking full-back, he'd played 277 games for Manchester, 33 for England, and been captain of both. Age: 28.

Eddie Colman
A midfield player who could pop and score vital goals, Eddie was a livewire joker. Age: only 21.

Duncan Edwards
A powerhouse midfield player who could attack or defend, he'd played his first League game at the age of 16 and won the first of his 18 caps for England when he was 18. Age: still only 21.

Mark Jones
A strong-tackling central defender. Age: just 24.

David Pegg
A left winger who'd made his debut for United at the age of 17 and had just played his first game for England. Age: only 22.

Tommy Taylor

Centre-forward for both Manchester United and England. One of the few players Matt Busby had bought, he'd cost a then record £29,999 – because Taylor himself preferred not to be in the spotlight as the first £30,000 player. Age: just 26.

Liam Whelan

Another goal-scoring forward, he'd started off that season with a hat trick on the opening day. Age: 23.

Another two United players, Jackie Blanchflower (aged 24) and Johnny Berry (aged 31), survived the crash but were so badly injured they never played again.

Question: Are you a Manchester United fan?
a) You bet!
b) Never in a million years!

Answer: It really doesn't matter.

Whether you support Manchester United or not, 6 February 1958 was a terrible day for football. People who taunt present Manchester United teams with cries of "Munich" aren't football fans, they're football fools. In the Munich air crash, it wasn't only Manchester United who lost their star players; England lost them too – and, most important of all, so did the game of football.

There's a Munich Memorial at Manchester United's ground, Old Trafford. It's a lasting tribute to the triumphant team that died.

THE 1960s: TERRIFIC TOTTENHAM

TRIUMPHANT TIMETABLE
League Champions: 1960-61
FA Cup Winners: 1960-61, 1961-62
European Cup Winner's Cup
Winners: 1962-63

Some teams are triumphant for years and years and years. Others sparkle for just a few golden seasons. And so, although Matt Busby produced another majestic Manchester United team (becoming the first English side to win the European Champions Cup in 1968), the vote for the team of the 1960s goes to Tottenham Hotspur.

WE'RE SO GOOD, PERHAPS WE SHOULD CHANGE OUR NAME TO MANCHESTER UNITED

Ever since the victorious Villa side of the 1890s no team in the twentieth century had managed to pull off the "Double" of winning both the League Championship and the FA Cup in the same season. Terrific Tottenham's claim to fame is that in the first full season of the 1960s they did it!

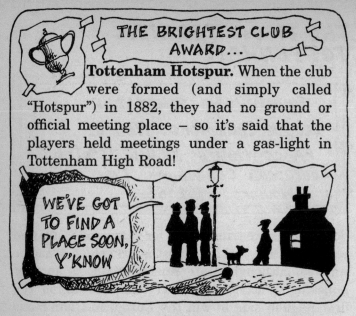

THE BRIGHTEST CLUB AWARD...

Tottenham Hotspur. When the club were formed (and simply called "Hotspur") in 1882, they had no ground or official meeting place – so it's said that the players held meetings under a gas-light in Tottenham High Road!

WE'VE GOT TO FIND A PLACE SOON, Y'KNOW

Many people were starting to believe that doing the Double was no longer possible.

AFTER ALL, THE LEAGUE WAS MUCH SMALLER IN THE DAYS OF PRESTON AND ASTON VILLA. TEAMS DIDN'T HAVE TO PLAY SO MANY MATCHES TO CAUSE THEM DOUBLE TROUBLE

NEWCASTLE UTD 1904-5 SUNDERLAND 1912-13 MANCHESTER UTD 1956-57

LOOK AT THE TRIUMPHANT TEAMS WHO'VE WON THE LEAGUE BUT RUN OUT OF STEAM AND LOST THE CUP FINAL!

But then the 1960–61 season began.

Tottenham won their first game. Then their second. Then their third. And their fourth, and their fifth…

Question: How many matches did Tottenham win in a row?
a) 7
b) 9
c) 11

Here's the triumphant Tottenham tally:
- They were top of the League from start to finish.
- They won the League by eight points.
- They scored 115 goals.
- They won 31 of their 42 games (still a record).
- They conceded only one penalty all season.
- They had only one player booked all season ... and none sent off.

THE TEAM LEAST LIKELY TO MAKE THE REFEREE'S PENCIL WEAR OUT AWARD...

Tottenham Hotspur, whose 1960–61 achievement of not having a player sent off was only a small part of a much prouder achievement. They hadn't had a player sent off in any game since Cecil Poynton on 27 October 1928 ... and didn't have one sent off until striker Jimmy Greaves got his marching orders on 24 April 1963 – nearly 35 years later! And who let Greaves into the dressing room for his early bath? Spurs' trainer, a former player named Cecil Poynton!

With the League Championship won, Spurs then sprinted to victory in the FA Cup Final as well, beating Leicester City 2-0.

So the Double-doubters had been demolished. By proving it was possible to win both competitions in the same season Spurs led the way for other triumphant teams like Arsenal (1970–71 and 1997–98), Liverpool (1985–86) and Manchester United (1993–94, 1995–96, 1998–99) to follow.

The following season, 1961–62, they managed what the "Busby Babes" of Manchester United had done and reached the semi-final of the European Champions Cup. They also won the FA Cup again, which put them into the European Cup Winners' Cup the following season.

No British side had yet won a European club competition. Rangers of Scotland having come nearest, reaching the final of the Cup Winners' Cup in 1962. So when Spurs played their way into the 1963 final against Atletico Madrid of Spain, and whacked them 5-1, they'd made history again!

The newspapers summed it all up neatly. Tottenham Hotspur weren't nicknamed "Spurs" any more. They were *Super* Spurs!

Main Men

Tottenham had a whole team full of great players. Some were tough, some were tricky – and one was a talker!

Dave Mackay

Dave was tough. How tough? Very tough! In December 1963, he broke his leg defending the European Cup Winners' Cup against the FA Cup holders Manchester United. Ten months later, fighting his way back in a reserve match, he broke the same leg again!

And yet who was the Spurs captain when they went on to beat Chelsea in the 1967 FA Cup Final? Dave Mackay.

Jimmy Greaves

Jimmy was tricky. Ask any defender who played against him! In his career he scored 357 League goals, every single one of them in the top division. One of his most amazing records is that he scored in the first game he played for every one of his clubs

(Chelsea, AC Milan of Italy, Spurs and West Ham) and the same goes for his England appearances too. Of them all, his debut game for Spurs was the best – he scored a hat trick!

Danny Blanchflower

The Spurs captain was an Irishman, and a great talker. He was the first to realize just how good the Spurs team were, and he was the first to say so, too...

THE DOUBLE WILL BE DONE—AND SPURS WILL BE THE TEAM TO DO IT!

That's what he prophesied in 1958, three years before it happened!

Talking came naturally to Blanchflower. What's more, he talked sense. Barnsley were his first professional club after leaving Ireland. There he'd been amazed to discover that most of the Barnsley training was done without a football in sight. When he asked why, he was told that if he didn't see a ball during the week then he'd be wanting to see more of it on a Saturday. But Danny replied:

IF I DON'T SEE THE BALL DURING THE WEEK, HOW WILL I KNOW WHAT IT LOOKS LIKE ON SATURDAY?

At Spurs, Blanchflower was always at the centre of the action. He was the man who speeded things up or slowed them down – and he did it so well that he was voted Footballer of the Year twice, in 1958 and 1961. Did it give him a big head? Not a bit of it...

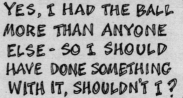

YES, I HAD THE BALL MORE THAN ANYONE ELSE – SO I SHOULD HAVE DONE SOMETHING WITH IT, SHOULDN'T I?

THE MOST UN-BIG-HEADED STAR PLAYER OFF THE FIELD AS WELL AS ON IT AWARD...

Danny Blanchflower. The TV programme *This Is Your Life* had secretly lined up Danny Blanchflower as the subject of one programme. The cameras were ready and all the guests assembled, but when the programme's presenter jumped out the modest Blanchflower took one look at the big red book under his arm ... and ran away! The programme was never made.

DANNY BLANCHFLOWER, THIS IS YOUR... 'ERE! WHERE'D HE GO?

As a player, Blanchflower had led Northern Ireland to the quarter-finals of the 1958 World Cup, and after retiring he became manager of Northern Ireland for a while. He knew they were never going to be world-beaters though, and sometimes made a joke of it, saying of his team's tactics:

WE TRY TO EQUALIZE BEFORE THE OTHER TEAM HAVE SCORED!

Above all, Danny Blanchflower believed that football should be played in a certain way.

FOOTBALL IS ABOUT GLORY, DOING THINGS IN STYLE, DOING THEM WITH A FLOURISH; IT'S ABOUT GOING OUT TO BEAT THE OTHER LOT, NOT WAITING FOR THEM TO DIE OF BOREDOM!

Super Spurs became a triumphant team by following their captain's orders!

THE TEMPESTUOUS TIMES QUIZ

A further batch of questions now, this time for the period 1940–1969. Can you score well?

1 In 1941, as the Second World War raged, Rome Radio announced that Arsenal's flying winger Cliff Bastin had been captured and was being held as a prisoner of war in Italy. True or false?

2 Wolverhampton Wanderers' Billy Wright was chosen as captain of England for the first time in 1948 – but he didn't hear it from the FA first. Who did tell him?

A HIS MUM

B WOLVES' GROUNDSMAN

C A BUS CONDUCTOR

3 During the 1947–48 season, every Manchester United fan went to watch games at Manchester City's ground instead. True or false?

4 "Gentleman" Jimmy Dickinson played a big part in winning the League for his team Portsmouth in their final game of the 1949–50 season. Needing to win their final game against Aston Villa, Portsmouth were awarded a free kick. Dickinson ran in and … what?

a) Smashed the ball into the net.

b) Pretended to smash the ball into the net.

c) Pretended to smash the ball into the net – then smashed the ball into the net.

5 In the 1950s and 1960s brothers Danny and Jackie Blanchflower were top players with Tottenham and Manchester United respectively. How had they practised their skills as youngsters?

A WITH BALLOONS

B WITH BUNDLES OF RAGS

C WITH NEWSPAPERS

6 Complete this saying by Bill Shankly, who became manager of Liverpool in 1959 and led them to triumph throughout the 1960s:

IF XXXXXXX WERE PLAYING AT THE BOTTOM OF MY GARDEN, I'D DRAW THE CURTAINS

7 In July 1964 John White, a key player of the 1960–61 double-winning Tottenham Hotspur team, was tragically killed by lightning at the age of 26 as he sheltered beneath a tree on a golf course. In the circumstances his nickname was really unfortunate. It was "The Ghost". True or false?

8 The Charity Shield match of 1967, between FA Cup winners Tottenham Hotspur and League Champions Manchester United, was an entertaining game that ended in a 3-3 draw. But at one point during the match Pat Jennings, the Spurs goalkeeper, expected the referee to penalize him. What for?

a) Scoring a goal.
b) Taking a free-kick.
c) Saving a penalty.

Answers: 1 True ... but it was a lie! The story had been made up in the hope of demoralizing the British soldiers with the news that one of their sporting heroes had been captured. The truth was that Bastin had hearing problems and wasn't fit enough to be a soldier. He spent the war on top of Highbury's main stand as a lookout! **2c)** The conductor had just seen it in the Stop Press column of a newspaper. **3 True** United's ground, Old Trafford, had been damaged by bombs during the war, so United played their home games at Manchester City's ground, Maine Road, instead. **4b)** He feinted, the Villa wall moved, and Portsmouth's Duggie Reid followed up to smash the ball into the net. Dickinson's Portsmouth went on to flatten Villa 6-1 and take the League title for the second season in a row. **5c)** They dribbled a ball around the streets as they delivered them on their paper rounds! **6** Everton (of course!). **7 True** White had been a cross-country champion and earned his nickname by having the ability race into goal-scoring positions at the very last moment so that – to defenders – it seemed as if he'd appeared out of nowhere! **8a)** Jennings had punted the ball miles downfield, seen it take one bounce – then sail over the head of Manchester United's goalkeeper Alex Stepney and into the net. He wasn't sure of the rules and was half-expecting the referee to blow his whistle and disallow the goal for some reason!

THE 1970s: LETHAL LEEDS

TRIUMPHANT TIMETABLE
League Champions: 1968-69, 1973-74
  FA Cup Winners: 1971-72
League Cup Winners: 1967-68
Fairs Cup Winners: 1967-68, 1970-71

During the 1960s and early part of the 1970s, Leeds United were a really successful triumphant team.

Unfortunately, though, their team were even more successful at being a nearly-triumphant team...

Nearly Triumphant Timetable
2nd in League: 1964-65, 1965-66,
1969-70, 1970-71, 1971-72
Losing FA Cup Finalists: 1964-65,
1969-70, 1972-73
Losing European Champions
Finalists: 1974-75
Losing European Cup Winners
Cup Finalists: 1972-73
Losing Fairs Cup Finalists:
1966-67

Even more unfortunately, it was quite often only the Leeds fans who were sad about this terrible run of near-misses. Most others were delighted! That's because lethal Leeds may have been a triumphant team but, until they changed their ways in the 1970s, they had a nasty habit of being a terrible team as well...

Triumphant! In 1964–65, Leeds' first season in the First Division after being promoted, they almost did the Double! They finished runners-up in the League and lost to Liverpool in the FA Cup Final. The team had changed their strip from yellow-and-blue to all-white shirts because their

manager, Don Revie, hoped they'd play like the five-times European Champions Real Madrid who played in all-white and had won the European Cup every year from 1956 to 1960! Well, Leeds had already gone a long way towards it – they'd made a lot of the other teams *real* mad!

Terrible! During their match against Manchester United, Leeds' midfield player Bobby Collins had given United's winger George Best a mighty kick in the leg. Then he'd growled, "That's just for starters, Bestie." What was so terrible about that? The game hadn't even started and the two teams were simply walking down the players' tunnel towards the pitch!

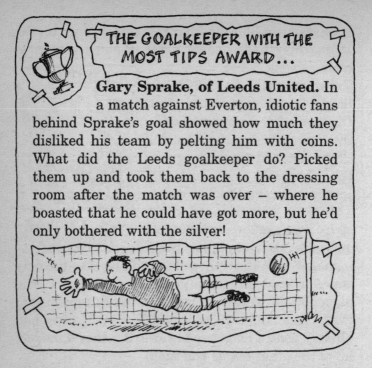

THE GOALKEEPER WITH THE MOST TIPS AWARD...

Gary Sprake, of Leeds United. In a match against Everton, idiotic fans behind Sprake's goal showed how much they disliked his team by pelting him with coins. What did the Leeds goalkeeper do? Picked them up and took them back to the dressing room after the match was over – where he boasted that he could have got more, but he'd only bothered with the silver!

Triumphant! In 1968–69 Leeds became League Champions, breaking all sorts of records on the way. They'd lost only two games all season, and (until it was later beaten by Liverpool in 1978–79) clocked up a record 67 points to beat that set by awesome Arsenal in 1930–31. One other record wasn't so impressive. In *their* record year, Arsenal had scored 127 goals but Leeds only scored a measly 66! (They thus became the first team ever to score more points than goals.)

Terrible! Leeds were experts at notching up 1-0 wins. Once they were ahead they would try to make certain the other team didn't score an equalizer. Wasting time was a favourite tactic.

Question: How did they like to do this?

| BY KICKING THE BALL OUT OF THE GROUND | BY KICKING THE BALL-BOYS OUT OF THE GROUND |

Answer: b) It was the job of the ball boys round the ground to run and fetch the ball whenever it went out of play. But if Leeds went 1-0 ahead, they'd all mysteriously disappear!

LEEDS HAVE SCORED!

OH, NO! NOT AGAIN!

YANK!

Nearly Treble triumphant! 1969–70 was the season Leeds United's hopes of total Treble triumph turned topsy-turvy. Until the very end of the season they were in the running for three titles: the League, the FA Cup and the European Champions Cup. But...

● They came second in the League to Everton.
● They lost to Scottish Champions Celtic in the European Cup semi-final.
● They lost to Chelsea in the FA Cup Final, after a replay.

It was a season that had finished in April to give England extra time to prepare for the World Cup in Mexico, and Leeds had been forced to play loads of games in a short space of time.

Question: Did they get much sympathy?

Answers: No! Not from the Football League, anyhow. When Leeds realized they couldn't win the League, they decided to rest their weary players and sent out a reserve side to face Derby. The team lost 1-4 ... and Leeds were heavily fined!
Yes! From Bill Shankly, manager of rivals Liverpool, who said:

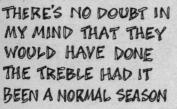 

THERE'S NO DOUBT IN MY MIND THAT THEY WOULD HAVE DONE THE TREBLE HAD IT BEEN A NORMAL SEASON

No! They didn't get much sympathy from one of the Chelsea players in the Cup Final that year, either. Maybe because Leeds' terrible streak was still going strong...

"There were eight or nine of them saying, 'Come over here and I'll break your leg,' and 'You go past me and you won't do it again.' But as soon as you started giving it back to them they'd say, 'Referee! Referee!' Oh, they were terrible."

Ian Hutchinson, Chelsea

Not quite triumphant again

In 1970–71, Leeds set a League record they really didn't want. They ended with 64 points, the most points any team had scored without actually winning the title. (They only came second.) Arsenal were League Champions that year with 65 points, and went on to win the FA Cup for the first Double since Terrific Tottenham ten years previously.

Terrible Terraces That season it was the lethal Leeds *fans* who caused trouble. When their team lost a crucial match 1-2 at home to West Bromwich Albion, with one of the West Brom goals being clearly offside, a group of them invaded the pitch and tried to grab the referee...

THE TRY TO HELP THE REFEREE EVEN THOUGH YOU WANT TO WRING HIS NECK AWARD...

Leeds United. After the controversial goal was scored, the whole Leeds team surrounded the poor referee and yelled at him. When their supporters came charging up to join in the action they decided they'd better stop and protect the referee instead!

IS IT SAFE TO COME OUT?

As a result of the pitch invasion Leeds were made to play their first four home games of the following season on a neutral ground. They dropped two points they might have gained if they'd been playing at home ... and lost the League by one point!

Triumphant ... and terribly disappointed! In 1971–72 Leeds won the FA Cup for the first time in their history and two days later would have won the Double if they could have scraped a draw in their last League match (away to Wolves). They lost 2-1.

Truly Triumphant! In 1973–74 Leeds United showed they could play football without being terrible. As the season reached October they were unbeaten; and they were still unbeaten in November; then December, then January... It wasn't until 23 February that they lost their first game! They'd gone a record 29 games unbeaten, and went on to become League Champions.

Truly Terrible! Leeds had qualified for the European Champions Cup again. Manager Don Revie had left to become England manager in 1974 but under their new boss, Jimmy Armfield, they battled their way through to the Final, and a match against Bayern Munich of West Germany. But it was to be another terrible time. Leeds had a "goal" disallowed, Bayern won 2-0 ... and the Leeds fans rioted again.

This time the club was banned from European competition for four years, and seven years later they were back in the Second Division.

Main Men

Leeds United's main men were a mix of the triumphant and terrible as well...

Jack Charlton

Otherwise known as "The Giraffe" because of his long neck and heading ability, Jack was their star defender. He played 629 games for Leeds, as well as being a member of the England team who won the World Cup in 1966.

He had a terrible tactic, though – at least, that's what opposing goalkeepers thought about it. Try it in the playground if you think you can get away with it...

● Wait till your team gets a corner kick.
● Trot upfield and into the other team's penalty area.
● Stand in front of their goalkeeper so that he can't see the ball.
● If the goalkeeper moves so that he can see, you move again so that he *can't*!
● Keep doing this until the corner is taken and, hopefully, headed past the poor goalkeeper and into the net!

Charlton was a tough competitor at his own end of the pitch, too. If somebody kicked him, he didn't forget. He once got in trouble for revealing that...

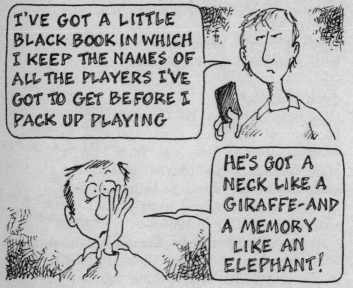

I'VE GOT A LITTLE BLACK BOOK IN WHICH I KEEP THE NAMES OF ALL THE PLAYERS I'VE GOT TO GET BEFORE I PACK UP PLAYING

HE'S GOT A NECK LIKE A GIRAFFE-AND A MEMORY LIKE AN ELEPHANT!

Billy Bremner

Voted Footballer of the Year in 1970, Billy was captain of both Leeds and Scotland. He was short in height (just 5 ft 4 inches, or 1.63m) and his temper was even shorter! Setting records with Leeds gave him plenty of triumphs, but there was nothing triumphant about one record he set. In 1974, together with Liverpool's Kevin Keegan, he became the first Briton to be sent off at Wembley!

It happened in the Charity Shield game that takes place every year between the League Champions and the FA Cup holders.

Warning: Do NOT try this in the playground!

LEEDS' JOHNNY GILES TACKLED KEEGAN FROM BEHIND...

BOOT!

KEEGAN HIT THE GROUND

THUD!

BREMNER RACED UP AND ACCUSED KEEGAN OF DIVING...

KEEGAN PUNCHED BREMNER...

BREMNER PUNCHED KEEGAN...

THE REF SENT THEM BOTH OFF!

'OP IT!

Question: Keegan was joined in the Wembley dressing room by his dad, who'd been watching the match. The two were sitting there feeling miserable when Billy Bremner knocked on the door. What happened next?

a) Bremner started fighting Keegan again.

b) Bremner started fighting with Keegan's dad.

c) Bremner apologized.

Bremner was a main man for Leeds because he always wanted to win. That much was obvious when his autobiography was published. It was called: *You Get Nowt For Being Second.*

THE 1980s: LORDLY LIVERPOOL

Liverpool's claim to fame is simple. They've had the most triumphant teams in English football – ever! So although Nottingham Forest had a great team at about that time (they won the European Champions Cup two years in a row in 1978–79 and 1979–80) the vote for the triumphant team of the 1980s goes to Liverpool.

In fact, they could well have been voted the team of the 1960s and 1970s as well! Liverpool had spent years struggling to get out of the Second Division, but once manager Bill Shankly had led them into the First Division in 1962, they were a teeny-weeny bit triumphant in the remainder of the 1960s...

LIVERPOOL'S 1960s TRIUMPHANT TIMETABLE
League Champions: 1963-64, 1965-66
FA Cup Winners: 1964-65

One of the keys to Liverpool's success was that their team hardly ever changed. A reporter once asked Bill Shankly: "What's the team, Bill?" He answered: "Same as last year."

Shankly was always building up his players to believe in themselves. If his team got beaten he would say about the other team: "Luck! They were rubbish! They'll never beat us again." But when Liverpool won he would tell his team, "They were brilliant, a great team. And you beat them, boys!"

It worked, too. Most of Shankly's players went on to become internationals – players like Ian Callaghan, Ray Clemence, Roger Hunt and Kevin Keegan of England, Ian St John and Ron Yeats of Scotland, John Toshack of Wales and Steve Heighway of the Republic of Ireland. In fact, Liverpool had so many star players that Shankly would sometimes leave their dressing-room door open slightly so that when the opposition arrived they'd see who they had to play against and be a bag of nerves before the game even began!

Tommy Smith of Liverpool. Smith was the triumphantly tough-tackling toughie of Shankly's teams. One of his more gentle games must have been for Liverpool Reserves against Preston Reserves, because the parents of the young Preston forward Smith had been marking came up to him after the match and said, "We would just like to shake your hand and thank you for not kicking our son!"

In the 1970s Liverpool improved. They weren't just a teeny-weeny bit triumphant – they were tremendously triumphant!

LIVERPOOL's 1970s TRIUMPHANT TIMETABLE

League Champions: 1972-73, 1975-76, 1976-77, 1978-79

FA Cup Winners: 1973-74

European Champions Cup Winners: 1976-77, 1977-78

UEFA Cup Winners: 1972-73, 1975-76

European Super Cup Winners: 1976-77

1972 saw the real beginning of an amazing spell. Between then and 1991, Liverpool were either Champions or runners-up in the League every year but one! (The odd year out was 1980–81, when they finished a measly fifth!)

In 1974, after leading his team to Wembley and a 3-0 FA Cup Final win against Newcastle United, Bill Shankly retired. Some clubs fade when their manager goes. But not Liverpool. When Shankly's assistant, Bob Paisley, took over they did the opposite – they got even better!

BRING BACK BILL SHANKLY!

● They became League Champions three more times. In 1978–79 their defence gave away a miserly 16 goals, a record low for a 42-game season.

● They had their first successes in Europe, winning the UEFA Cup in 1972–73 and again in 1975–76.
● Even better, they went on to win the European Champions Cup in 1976–77, then became the first British club to lift it twice in a row when they did the trick again the following season.

Liverpool perfected triumphant tactics for two-leg European matches, which needed a strong performance at home, but patient passing and defending away. In one UEFA Cup game against Barcelona they were winning 1-0 in Spain. Suddenly the crowd started misbehaving, throwing sweets and cushions down towards the pitch.

Some of them landed near the Liverpool reserve, Joey Jones, who was sitting on the bench with manager Bob Paisley.

Question: What did Jones do?

a) He grabbed a cushion and sat on it.

b) He grabbed some sweets and began munching them.

c) He leaped up and started throwing them back at the crowd.

Answer: c) Jones was furious because he thought the crowd were throwing things at them – until manager Paisley grabbed him and packed him off to the dressing room, pointing out that throwing things was how Spanish spectators abuse a team who weren't playing well enough to get a kick. The crowd were lobbing their missiles at the Barcelona players!

THE MOST HIGHLY POWERED SHIRTS AWARD...

Liverpool FC who in July 1979 became the first club to carry a sponsor's name on the front of their shirts. It was Hitachi, the huge Japanese electronics company. No wonder visiting teams always seemed to be in a state of shock after playing Liverpool!

And so to the 1980s, the decade which saw Liverpool become totally triumphant – but which also ended in tears...

```
LIVERPOOL'S 1980s TRIUMPHANT TIMETABLE
League Champions: 1979-80, 1981-82,
1982-83, 1983-84, 1985-86, 1987-88, 1989-90
FA Cup Winners: 1985-86, 1988-89
League Cup Winners: 1980-81, 1981-82,
   1982-83, 1983-84
European Champions Cup Winners:
   1980-81, 1983-84
```

- Liverpool begin the decade with another League Championship. They introduce different players along the way, but none have as dramatic an opening game as Israeli international Avi Cohen. He makes his debut for Liverpool against Aston Villa, in a game that will make Liverpool Champions if they win, and scores after 25 minutes! Unfortunately, it's an own goal! Twenty-five minutes later he scores again – but this time it's at the right end as he makes the score 2-1 to Liverpool. The team go on to triumph 4-1.
- At the end of the 1982–83 season Liverpool suffer a dramatic loss of form. They don't win one of their last seven games, losing five and only drawing two. So did they finish well down the table? No, they'd been so far ahead of everybody

else they'd virtually won the Championship before their sad sequence started.

● Also in 1982–83, they become the first team to win every one of the English trophies by winning the League Cup against Manchester United at Wembley. At the end of the game the Liverpool players pull off another first. What is it?

(a) THEY DO A LAP OF HONOUR BEFORE RECEIVING THE CUP!

WHO'S GOT THE CUP?

(b) THEY SEND MANAGER BOB PAISLEY UP TO COLLECT THE TROPHY

AND WHICH POSITION DO YOU PLAY?

(c) THEY THROW THEIR MEDALS TO THE LIVERPOOL FANS

I'LL PUT IT WITH MY TIDDLY-WINKS MEDAL

Answer: b) It's Bob Paisley's last season as manager, so the players push him up the steps to the royal box and make him the first manager to receive a trophy at Wembley.

● Just as Bill Shankly's job had been taken over by his assistant Bob Paisley, so Paisley's place is taken by *his* assistant, Joe Fagan ... and in Fagan's first year as manager, 1983–84, Liverpool win three trophies: the League, the League Cup and the European Champions Cup! The League

133

win is their third in a row, achieving what only Huddersfield and Arsenal had done before them. And, in the League Cup, they beat their Liverpool neighbours and arch-rivals Everton after a replay, seeming to prove what Bill Shankly had always said... *"There are two great teams in Liverpool: Liverpool – and Liverpool Reserves!"*

THE NOISIEST MANAGER AWARD...

Joe Fagan of Liverpool. The night before their European Champions Cup Final in Rome, against Italian team Roma, Liverpool team-mates Kenny Dalglish and Graeme Souness found themselves kept awake by a radio blaring out from the room next door. Souness was ready to go round and sort out the culprit, but Dalglish persuaded him to ring the hotel's receptionists and ask them to fix things. Just as well – the players discovered next morning that the radio rowdy in the next room was their own manager!

BOOM! BOOM! BOOM!

● Then the tears begin. In 1984–85, Liverpool reach the European Champions Cup Final again. They're playing the Italian club, Juventus, at the small Heysel Stadium in Brussels, Belgium. But before the game gets under way, some hooligans amongst the Liverpool fans break down fences and charge the Juventus section. There's a panic, a wall collapses, and 38 people – mostly Juventus fans – die. To prevent further trouble the game is still played. Liverpool lose 1-0, but nobody really cares. Afterwards, English clubs are banned from European competitions for several years with an extra-long ban for Liverpool. Their European triumphs are over.

- The team are still triumphant in England, though. The following season, 1985–86, new manager (but still a player) Kenny Dalglish outdoes all the previous Liverpool managers and leads his team to the League and FA Cup Double. And who do they beat 3-1 at Wembley to clinch the Double? Everton!

- Much to the disgust of everybody who thought Liverpool were good enough already, the team gets even better. In 1987–88 they equal Lethal Leeds' record of remaining unbeaten for 29 matches from the start of the season. Could they go one better? No, they couldn't. In their 30th match they're beaten 0-1 ... by Everton! Liverpool have the last laugh, though. They become League Champions yet again.

THE ONLY WAY TO BEAT LIVERPOOL IS TO LET THE BALL DOWN !

ALAN BALL (EX-EVERTON PLAYER)

- 1988–89 is a season of triumph and tragedy. The League Championship is won by Arsenal in an epic match at Anfield, just days after Liverpool had beaten Everton (again!) 3-2 at Wembley to win the FA Cup. But none of this could go anywhere near making up for the tragedy which had taken place at the FA Cup semi-final. Late-arriving spectators had mistakenly been let into an already packed section behind one goal. Those at the front had been crushed down against the fences round the pitch which had been erected in the first place precisely because of the sort of hooliganism seen at Heysel in Belgium. Ninety-five fans of all ages died through suffocation. Manager Kenny Dalglish summed up the tragedy by saying, *"Football is irrelevant now."*
- Liverpool were crowned League Champions yet again the following season, 1989–90 … but manager Dalglish resigned shortly after. It was to be the last title in a remarkable run.

Main Men

Even before the foreign invasion of the 1990s many of Liverpool's star players weren't English. In fact the first team ever to take the field for Liverpool only contained one Englishman, their goalkeeper. All the other ten outfield players were Scots.

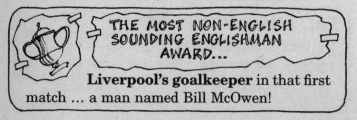

THE MOST NON-ENGLISH SOUNDING ENGLISHMAN AWARD…

Liverpool's goalkeeper in that first match … a man named Bill McOwen!

Nothing much had changed by 1986. That year Liverpool regularly fielded a team with only player born in England – Mark Lawrenson ... and even he played for the Republic of Ireland! (Because of the nationality of his grandparents.)

So out of the many great players to wear a Liverpool shirt here are a Scot, a Welshman – and a clumsy goalkeeper...

Bruce Grobbelaar

Bruce played for Liverpool throughout the triumphant 1980s and, not surprisingly, won more honours than any other goalkeeper.

Question: What was his job before he became a professional footballer?
a) A soldier.
b) A gambler.
c) A lawyer.

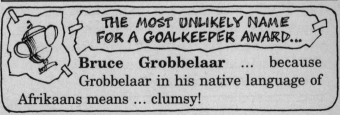

Answer: a) ... in the army of Rhodesia (now Zimbabwe), in the southern part of Africa.

THE MOST UNLIKELY NAME FOR A GOALKEEPER AWARD...
Bruce Grobbelaar ... because Grobbelaar in his native language of Afrikaans means ... clumsy!

137

Grobbelaar was thought of by the Liverpool fans as Bruce the Brilliant – usually. He could make stunning saves one minute and horrible howlers the next. But he was always entertaining. He would often prowl round his penalty area on his hands!

Ian Rush

Welsh wizard Ian Rush was Liverpool's ace goalscorer in the 1980s. He joined the club in 1980, left for a year to play for Italian club Juventus, then came back again in 1988 and stayed until 1996. With a total of 233 goals in 469 games, he broke records nearly as often as defenders' hearts – especially Everton

defenders! Rush scored five goals in FA Cup Finals, more than any other player, and four of them were in Liverpool's victories over their arch-rivals in 1986 and 1989.

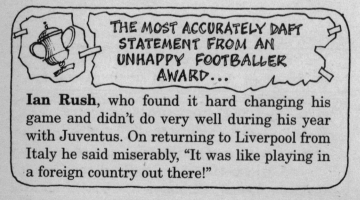

THE MOST ACCURATELY DAFT STATEMENT FROM AN UNHAPPY FOOTBALLER AWARD...

Ian Rush, who found it hard changing his game and didn't do very well during his year with Juventus. On returning to Liverpool from Italy he said miserably, "It was like playing in a foreign country out there!"

Kenny Dalglish

Dalglish was nicknamed "King Kenny" by the Liverpool fans because before he became a triumphant Liverpool manager he'd been a triumphant Liverpool player.

Question: On 26 November 1983, Dalglish managed a really rare scoring feat. What was it?
a) He scored with a header from outside the penalty area.
b) He scored a hat trick of penalties.
c) He scored 100 goals for both an English and a Scottish club.

Answer: c) On that day Dalglish scored his 100th goal for Liverpool, matching the 100+ he'd scored for his previous club, Celtic.

During his playing career he was also joint top-scorer for Scotland, with 30 goals in a record 102 appearances. In fact, if Dalglish aimed, he very rarely missed ... except for once, in the 1982–83 League Cup Final. The match had gone into extra time and Liverpool, 2-1 up, were being hard pressed by their opponents, Manchester United. Dalglish got the ball and decided to try and waste a bit of time.

Question: What did he do?
a) He hit the ball into the stands.
b) He dribbled the ball to the corner flag and stood on it.
c) He aimed to drop it down a hole.

Answer: c) The hole in question was the players' tunnel. Dalglish aimed, but missed! All worked out well in the end, though. Liverpool hung on to win.

THE 1990s: MAJESTIC MANCHESTER UNITED II

TRIUMPHANT TIMETABLE

Premier League Champions: 1992-93, 1993-94, 1995-96, 1996-97, 1998-99, 1999-2000

FA Cup Winners: 1989-90, 1993-94, 1995-96, 1998-99

League Cup Winners: 1991-92

European Champions Cup Winners: 1998-99

European Cup Winners' Cup Winners: 1990-91

Nobody could disagree that Manchester United were the most triumphant team of the 1990s...

● They did the Double in 1993–94.
● They did the Double again in 1995–96, becoming the first triumphant team to do the "double Double".

NOW THEY'VE DONE THE DOUBLE DOUBLE, I WONDER IF THEY'LL DO THE TREBLE DOUBLE?

YOU TALK DOUBLE DUTCH!

- They did it again in 1998–99 ... and added the European Champions Cup the same year to pull off a Treble triumph that no English club had ever managed before!

If you were born in the late 1980s or early 1990s, you've probably grown up expecting to see Manchester United right up at the top of the League table. But...

Question: Until their first title of the 1990s, in 1992–93, United hadn't been Champions since ... when?
a) 1976–77
b) 1966–67
c) 1956–57

Answer: b) In fact they'd been waiting even longer than their rivals Manchester City – City had won the League the season following United, in 1967–68!

United's manager Alex Ferguson (now Sir Alex) found out the news while playing a different sort of ball game. With his team ahead in the table, their closest rivals Aston Villa had to beat Oldham to stand any chance of catching United up. Rather than listen to the match on the radio, Ferguson went off for a game of golf instead.

He was on the last green when another golfer hurried up to him. "Excuse me, Mr Ferguson," he said. "Oldham have won at Aston Villa. You are the Champions."

Question: Even though they'd won the League, Manchester United weren't given the trophy won by the previous season's League Champions, Leeds United. Why not?

a) It had been stolen.

b) It had been damaged and was being mended.

c) It had been replaced by another one.

Answer: c) 1992–93 was the season the old First Division was renamed The FA Premiership. A new trophy had taken its place. It was bigger than the old one and had a crown for a lid – so that the winners could be "crowned" Champions. Yuk!

It was in 1995–96 that a lot of new, young players started to appear in the Manchester United line-up – players like David Beckham, Paul Scholes, Gary and Philip Neville. The season didn't begin well, though. United lost their first game and know-all ex-players rushed in with their views.

One of them was a member of the lordly Liverpool team of the 1980s, Alan Hansen, who famously said…

It's just as well Hansen was a good defender in his day, because nine months later he was having to defend what he'd said. Manchester United – complete with kids – had pulled off the League and FA Cup Double again!

THE MOST ENTERPRISING TACTIC FOR ATTRACTING YOUNG PLAYERS BEFORE THEY'RE EVEN OLD ENOUGH TO WALK AWARD...

Manchester United whose shop sells just about everything with the club badge on it – even a babygro carrying the message "Here We Grow!"

HE'S COMING ON FINE

In 1998–99, Manchester United pulled off nothing less than a Treble triumph.

LOOK! WE'VE WON A CUP FOR WINNING SO MANY CUPS!

- They won the League Championship by one point from Arsenal.
- They beat Newcastle United 2-0 to win the FA Cup.
- They beat German side Bayern Munich 2-1 to win the European Champions Cup.

But how many would they have won if the rules of the game, developed back in the days of the Wanderers, had said, "Matches will last for 89 minutes exactly."?

They certainly wouldn't have won the FA Cup. In the fourth round they were losing 1-0 to Liverpool with less than a minute to go ... but when the referee blew for full-time it was Liverpool who'd been knocked out. United had scored twice in a minute to win 2-1.

They wouldn't have won the European Champions Cup, either. In the final of that competition, Bayern Munich were 1-0 up after 90 minutes. They were playing injury time added on by the referee. But yet again, when the whistle went for full-time, Manchester United had scored two goals in the final minutes to win 2-1!

THE FORTUNE TELLER MOST TRIUMPHANTLY PERFORMING AS A TV COMMENTATOR AWARD...

Clive Tyldesley, commentating on the European Champions Cup Final as the game entered its final seconds with Manchester United, who'd scored in every match of the competition, still 0-1 down...

"They must score. They always score!"

Seconds later, they did.

Main Men

Apart from being one of the most triumphant teams, Manchester United are the best supported. They've got millions of followers all over the world. In school playgrounds from Manchester to Malaysia, would-be footballers are trying out the tricks they've seen their favourite Man U players perform on the TV.

Here are some of Manchester United's main men in the 1990s, and the tricks they've used. Copy those marked ☺ – but you can rightly expect a stack of detentions if you try any of those marked ☠.

Peter Schmeichel

Schmeichel was United's goalkeeper until 1999 and his favourite tricks both involved roaring.

He would roar rude words at any of his team-mates who he thought had made a mistake.

If Manchester United were losing in the final minutes and won a corner, Schmeichel would roar upfield and join the attack. In a UEFA cup-tie against the Russian side Rotor Volvograd in 1995–96 he actually scored with a header!

WHAT THE...

Ryan Giggs

Having been a regular in the United team since he was 17, Giggs has won more medals at a younger age than any other player.

He's also the holder of one unusual record – the only player to have represented two countries under different names: Ryan Giggs and Ryan Wilson. To do this yourself you'll have to be Welsh, go to a school in England, get picked for England schoolboys, turn out for them using your dad's surname (Wilson), then use your mum's surname for the rest of your life, especially when you get picked for Wales. Not easy.

In the fourth round of the FA Cup against Southampton in 1991–92, Manchester United became the first team to be knocked out of that competition using the new penalty shoot-out rule. And the player responsible for one of United's historic penalty misses was ... Ryan Giggs.

David Beckham

Becks was one of the young players Alex Ferguson turned to in 1995–96. Maybe you fancy being a professional footballer? Then you'll certainly have to impress a professional club in a trial match...

As a teenager, Beckham went for a trial with Tottenham Hotspur. His skills must have impressed them, but they couldn't have liked one thing about him. He turned up wearing a replica Manchester United shirt!

You can't try Beckham's best trick in the playground (not unless it's huge). You need to go out on to a full-size pitch and hold a match. Hang about in your own half, just inside the centre-circle. Then, when the ball comes near you, simply send it sailing all the way down to the other end, over the goalkeeper's head ... and into your opponent's net. That was how Beckham scored one of his most memorable goals, a 60-metre shot from inside his own half against Wimbledon in Manchester United's first game of the 1996–97 season.

Eric Cantona

French-born Eric was United's undisputed star from 1993 until he retired from the game (to be an actor!) at the end of the 1996–97 season. His spectacular career's got more 😇 than most, but a lot more 😈 too! There was never a dull moment when Eric was about...

😇 In 1983–88 Cantona begins his career with French club Auxerre.

😈 He's fined for giving a goalkeeper a black eye – his *own* goalie!

I DIDN'T SEE **THAT** SHOT COMING!

😇 In 1988–89 he wins a French Cup and League double with new club Marseilles.

😈 He's suspended for throwing his shirt at the referee after being substituted.

😇 In 1989–91 he has spells with four different clubs – Bordeaux, Montpellier, Marseilles (where he's a League title winner again) and Nîmes.

😈 He's transferred by Bordeaux for missing training, suspended at Montpellier for chucking his boots at a team-mate, injured for three months at Marseilles – but saves his worst for Nîmes. There he is banned for three games for throwing the ball in a referee's face, suspended for two months for assaulting an opponent ... and then tops it all off by calling the French League's disciplinary panel idiots!

In 1991–92 he joins Leeds and helps them to become League Champions!

He's transferred to Manchester United in November 1992 ... and is soon fined £1,000 for spitting at Leeds fans when he goes back to play their team.

In 1992–93 and 1993–4 he wins the League twice with Manchester United to give him four Championships in a row with three different teams!

In 1994, at the end of a European Champions Cup match in Turkey, he accuses the referee of accepting bribes. It's a bad move. If Cantona thinks the referee won't understand his French, then he's wrong – back home in Switzerland the ref's job is teaching French! Cantona is given a red card and ends up having a fight in the players' tunnel.

He also earns an FA Cup winners' medal in 1994, scoring two penalties in United's 4-0 triumph against Chelsea.

In January 1995 Cantona commits his worst offence yet. After he's sent off in a match against Crystal Palace a slob of a spectator launches into a frothing foul-mouthed scream stream ... so Cantona launches himself into a kung-fu kick at the spectator! He's fined big money, banned for eight months – and Manchester United win nothing that season.

Cantona is also taken to court and narrowly escapes being sent to gaol. Instead he's given the punishment of "community service". He spends 120 hours teaching youngsters how to play football – and does a brilliant job. When he returns to the Manchester United side for the 1995–96 season they do the Double again, with Cantona scoring the winning goal in the Cup Final against Liverpool.

There isn't one! Instead...

153

...the experience of working with enthusiastic youngsters seems to turn Eric the 'Ead-case into Cantona the Considerate. He's only booked once all season and ends up becoming the first overseas player to be voted Player of the Year in England!

Eric Cantona had one more surprise up his sleeve. After helping Manchester United to yet another League title in 1996–97 he announced that he was retiring from football altogether. He was going to become an actor.

THE MODERN GAME QUIZ

Here's your final chance to prove you're a towering triumph at answering tricky teasers: a batch of questions covering some of the pottier proceedings between 1970 and 2000.

1 Arsenal completed the Double in 1970–71 with a flower in goal! Keeper Bob Wilson's middle name is that of a flower. What is it? (Triumphant tip: he can be proper prickly about it!)

2 Not all top players retire at the top, some drop down the Leagues. Tottenham star Jimmy Greaves did this. He was playing for Barnet in 1977 when the referee sent him off in a match against Chelmsford. What happened next? (Triumphant tip: the ref didn't view it with gay abandon)

3 On 9 February 1979, Trevor Francis becomes Britain's first £1 million player. He joins Nottingham Forest from Birmingham City but isn't eligible to play for Forest when his new team reach the League Cup Final. His new manager, Brian Clough, finds him a job to do on the day of the big match though. What is it? (Triumphant tip: Francis still got to lift the cup)

4 In 1980, Coventry City cooked up a great sponsorship deal with a local car manufacturer named Talbot. Part of the deal is that the club changes its name to Coventry Talbot FC. What do the Football Association say? (Triumphant tip: the answer is either "Yes" or "No"!)

5 Violence in Scotland. In 1982 a player was banned for 30 years after assaulting a referee during a match in The Edinburgh _____ Sunday League. Fill in the missing word to complete the name of the League. (Triumphant tip: the whole incident caused a holy row)

6 On 13 April 1998 a match between Arsenal and Blackburn started with a white ball and ended with an orange ball. Why? (Triumphant tip: the players didn't mind; in fact you could say it was all-white by them)

7 It's 1999 and commercial deals for two footballers are signed and sealed. A company launches snacks with two new flavours – Salt & Lineker and Cheese & Owen. What type of snack is it? (Triumphant tip: both Lineker and Owen are famous for being snappy strikers)

8 England manager Kevin Keegan, TV comentating on the European Champions League match between

Manchester United and Fiorentina on 15 March 2000, passes a considered opinion on the performance of United's striker Andy Cole, saying:

COLE'S ON XXXX TONIGHT?

Fill in the missing word. (Triumphant tip: Cole was being given glowing praise)

CAN YOU SMELL BURNING?

Answers: 1 Primrose! (*prim* = proper and a *rose* is prickly, geddit!) **2** Greaves refused to leave the pitch, so the referee abandoned the match. **3** He's given the job of making the tea at half-time! **4** No ... and Coventry later breathe a sigh of relief when the Talbot company go bust! **5** The Edinburgh *Churches* Sunday League! **6** There was a snow storm at half-time. **7** Crisps. **8** Fire.

So who will be the triumphant team of the 2000s?

Will Manchester United majestically mangle all-comers? Will Liverpool lord it over everybody again? Or will Arsenal become awesome once more? Will it be Leeds who regain their lethal touch? Or Tottenham who turn terrific again? Perhaps Aston Villa will recover their victorious ways or Newcastle their niftiness?

Is it possible that triumphant teams of the past can surge back into the top division and be triumphant again? Can Preston recover their pride, Portsmouth their power, Blackburn their brilliance or Wolverhampton Wanderers become wonderful again?

You don't support any of these teams? No matter. Perhaps the 2000s will be a dynamic decade for the side you *do* support.

So cheer them on – they could be the next triumphant team!